LITTLE HIDDEN DOORS

LITTLE HIDDEN DOORS

a guided journal
for deep dreamers

NAOMI SANGREAL

STERLING ETHOS
New York

STERLING ETHOS
New York

ISBN 978-1-4549-4878-0

Library of Congress Control Number: 2023935325

For information about custom editions, special sales, and premium purchases, please contact specialsales@unionsquareandco.com.

Printed in China

2 4 6 8 10 9 7 5 3 1

unionsquareandco.com

Cover design by Jo Obarowski

Cover art © 2023 by Naomi Sangreal
Painting reference attributed to James Kerwin's photo: Interior of an abandoned building in Kolmannskuppe, Namibia licensed under CC by SA 2.0. https://commons.wikimedia.org/wiki/File:Abandoned_building,_Kolmannskuppe,_Namibia.jpg

Interior design by Stacy Wakefield Forte

Throughout: Shutterstock.com: Danussa (clouds and dunes); Sylverarts Vectors (page frame); collages by Naomi Sangreal

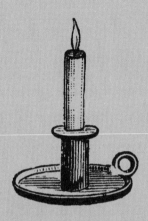

To my loving parents, who have
been recording my dreams
since I was a year old, never
ceasing to support my magic.

To my ancestors, bright
spirits who illuminate my
path and walk with me,
I honor you with every breath.

CONTENTS

ABOUT THIS BOOK

Little Hidden Doors is a guided journal for deep dreamers—a handbook packed with many ways to access the psyche through our dreams. Filled with useful information about the scientific and psychological phenomenon of dreams, visual meditations, original artwork, writing prompts, and invitations to create art, this journal is a powerful tool and vessel for dreamers to deepen their understanding of their dreams. It is a comprehensive introduction, extending across many dreamwork techniques and theories, which allows readers to find what resonates for them personally. It is a door, itself, filled with more doors leading to the inner reaches of ourselves and the places where we are a part of something bigger.

HOW TO USE THIS JOURNAL: This is the book that I have always wanted. A book that holds processes and particulars from the world of dreams. It emerged from my direct experience with the powerful psychological transformation that is possible when one attends to the magic of their dreaming mind. This book was born for our inner world to have a space, a transitional object, and a physical container to hold deep psyche's imagination. This journal occupies the versatile space of a unique intersection; it is an interactive tool for both the novice dreamer's inner work at home or on the road and the dreamwork clinician to use with clients as a psychological container within the context of therapy. It is a place for dreamers, psychotherapists, and their clients to learn about and document dreams in practice. Each chapter begins with a research-based introduction to a dreamwork concept or modality and subsequently offers some space to physically engage with the dream through writing prompts, journaling, and artistic process. This way the dreamer has the opportunity to integrate their knowledge through practice and directly witness the transformative power of working with their dreams over time.

For the clinician, this journal provides an adjunctive object that holds the client's psychic contents for work within a session. The clinician and client can together reflect on the client's dreams and their work within the book, closing its covers as a sacred container at the end of the session. As psychoanalyst Thomas Ogden expressed, "The patient's experience of being creative in the act of communicating is an essential part of the process of [their] 'dreaming [themself] more fully into existence,' coming into being in a way that is uniquely [their] own." Therapy that includes dreams, images, and active imagination can shed light on the shadowed parts of the self, supporting them in the co-creative dance of dreaming their unconscious contents into conscious reality for life-changing integration. Because dreams are able to communicate specific details from the unconscious through personal mythopoesis, they are incredibly useful for the dreamers' therapist to consider. Unveiling these rich and vibrant images through therapy can help the client access deeply troubling dynamics that are beyond the moderation and control of their ego and aid in facilitating psychic growth and healing. Dreaming is a door: let us open it.

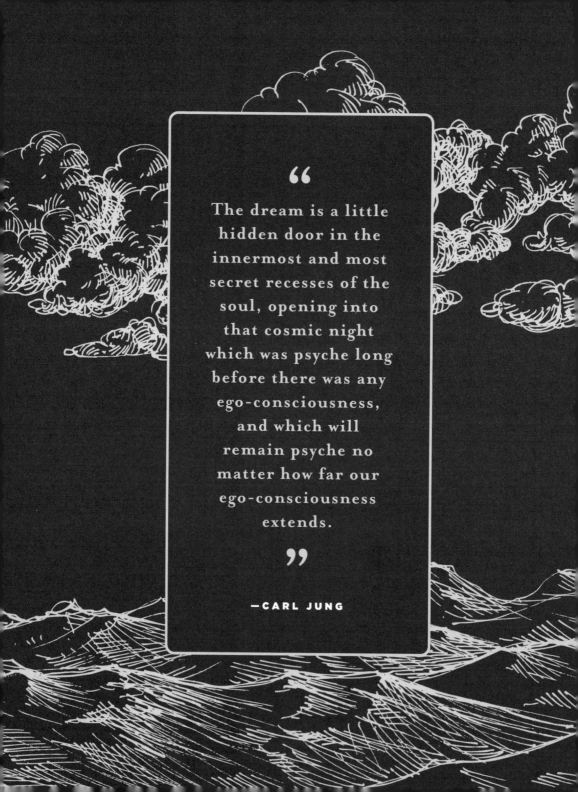

"

The dream is a little hidden door in the innermost and most secret recesses of the soul, opening into that cosmic night which was psyche long before there was any ego-consciousness, and which will remain psyche no matter how far our ego-consciousness extends.

"

—CARL JUNG

THROUGH DREAMS
I ARRIVED . . .

From a young age, I was an imaginative, deep, and visual soul, both an artist and an intuitive, and I have been a painter and a vivid dreamer for as long as I can remember. As the sensitive daughter of a psychotherapist and a social worker, my path felt clear from the beginning. My mother began recording my dreams at age one, and throughout my life, they have been a constant, powerful, and guiding force. As a child, I believed in the collective dream; I used to spend hours recounting my nightly adventures into a coil corded telephone, my best friend's ear pressed into its receiving end as we wove our dreams together. I imagined that this is what the ancients did around a raging fire at night, freeing the treasured images of their wild souls in beautiful dialects sounding across the flames, the sparks of speech illuminating fantastical landscapes and forming fervent conversation from shared dreams. When I told my best friend that in my dream I had opened a door, she responded by sharing a detailed synchronistic account of how, in her dream, she had serendipitously walked through it. From then on, I believed that whenever my dream ended, another's began.

A child inspired by meaning, I was drawn to exploring the mystical realms that stirred my connection to spirit and were expressed through my earliest artwork. My formal arts training as an adolescent through arts-focused magnet elementary and middle schools greatly nourished and expanded my artistic abilities. This led me into my creative young adulthood as a prolific painter. Around this time, I began taking lucid dreaming more seriously. I loved learning about dreaming and practicing ways to expand my dream experience. I especially loved to fly in my dreams (who doesn't?), a feeling incomparable to the gravity of the daily realities that high school offers. I scribbled small dream moments down in lined notebooks and on scraps of paper, and sometimes lines of poetry or a vivid image would emerge. After high school, I went on to receive a scholarship to attend the Pacific Northwest College of Art (PNCA). My experience there, as well as my involvement in the art world as an institution, revealed to me that my work was profoundly personal and driven by a need for raw expression, rather than commercial or public consumption. I focused my creativity inward, diving deeper into the depths of psyche and seeking my truest Self.

Human behavior and consciousness have always fascinated me, maybe it is my Aquarian nature, or my Pisces moon, but I have perpetually found myself enchanted by the otherworldly, non-ordinary and philosophical questions of life. After leaving art school, I sought to better understand myself, my experiences, and my artwork and decided to begin seeing a dream-focused Jungian psycho-therapist. Her name was Satya Byock, and she completely changed my life.

Dreams led me to therapy.

After years of psychotherapy, one day, I had a BIG dream. I brought it into our therapy session and followed its imaginal threads until it spoke to me in a loud, unwavering and incontestable voice. I knew then what I had to do. I decided to go back to school to study dreams and become a therapist in 2015. I studied for six years straight. Following my Masters in Counseling and Depth Psychology graduation in 2022, I began to write this book. Realizing the momentous effects of my personal therapy, dreamwork, and artistic practice has inspired me to share with others and perpetuate this form of learning, growing, and cultivating self-love through the creation of this sacred object, *Little Hidden Doors*, a guided journal for deep dreamers. Creativity is innate to the human experience and has been utilized since the dawn of time to express the ineffable. Even humans in ancient civilizations had the urge to make an object or experience something special, something beyond its common utilitarian purpose. In earlier cultures, art was often used as an integral part of ritual and in the worship of divine beings. It was and still is an intermediary medium connecting matter. As anthropologist Ellen Dissanayake said, "Since all human societies, past and present, so far as we know, make and respond to art, it must contribute something essential to human life and spirit."

Dreams are these beautiful strings of potent visualizations that we get during sleep. They are often misunderstood or regarded as meaningless, and frequently dismissed and thought of as unimportant. I have been doing dreamwork throughout most of my life, and currently work in private practice as a magical, Jungian, and depth psychology–oriented psychotherapist, where dreamwork is a central tenet of my therapeutic approach. I view dreams as raw expressions of the personal and collective unconscious, offering images that hold psyche's deep soul, raw and unencumbered. Dreams are incredibly packed with meaningful, rich, and wise material that you can work with to help guide your life.

Through my own creative practice and dreamwork, I have found access to aspects of Self and psychological transformation by sublimating dreams into physical art. As noted later, the Self is an innate and archetypal psychic system that organizes consciousness and magnetizes the numinous in service to our individual unique individuation process. My personal experience with dreamwork has been profound and continues throughout my creative dreaming practice. Reflecting on my own journey as an artist, dreamer, and psychotherapist has driven me to deepen my own relationship to these concepts and further realize their relevance within modern psychotherapy and personal healing. Witnessing the unfolding of this work will continue throughout the rest of my life, and it is my hope to contribute to the evolution of a potency in human creative consciousness that moves us toward what I feel is a great becoming. Enjoy!

wake-centricity

My passion for dreamwork and dream psychology initially developed based on several universal truths. First and foremost, humans across cultures—spiritual, indigenous, religious, and contemporary—have valued the phenomena of dreams. Traditions that have cultivated serious dream practices have learned how to go beyond the waking, conscious, egoic aspect of the psyche, and these practices have an immensely positive influence on their day-to-day lives. Historians, theologians, and psychologists alike acknowledge that dream practices have been integral to cultures all over the world for thousands of years. Yet dreams are still not often considered for their innately useful properties in contemporary Western societies. In the average human lifespan, a person devotes at least 50,000 hours to dreaming. That is almost six years of life spent within a dream! When considering the nature of consciousness, it is important to include this large fraction of our human experience, even though we may be conditioned not to. Neuroscientists and psychologists are willing to consider most human behavior that is in the same territory as dreams as meaningful in the same way that eating, sleeping, defecating, mating, and so forth would be. These are all basic and instinctual natural human processes, and dreaming is no different.

Although historically, dreams have served as templates for transmitting wisdom, within the context of America in the twenty-first century, dreams are generally not considered to be important. In modern American society, there seems to be loyalty to waking consciousness as the primary viable form of reality and experience. Often, the cultural narrative perpetuates the notion that "it was just a dream," which emerges across decades in song lyrics, movies, and modern media. As psychologist Rubin Naiman suggested, American cultural bias is "*wake-centric*" and views dreaming as "subservient to waking consciousness." This egocentric culture focused on productivity, a reified self, and waking existence often dismisses dream states because, from the vantage point of the ego, the waking conscious mind does not have the capacity to fully experience dream states.

In part, the lack of comprehension may be because dreams picture the unconscious condition in symbolic form—in images that point beyond themselves to the as-yet unknown or unknowable. Founder of analytical psychology Carl Jung wrote, "That dreams should have a meaning, and should therefore be capable of interpretation, is certainly neither a strange nor an extraordinary idea. It has been known to mankind for thousands of years; indeed it has become something of a truism." Dreamwork has been expressed by traditions all over the world as having intrinsic value and inherently healing properties; yet, curiously, modern America has largely failed to encourage individuals to engage with their dreams. American wake-centrism continues to perpetuate the consciousness divide and invalidate the power of dream-consciousness, which results in continual separation from a huge proportion of psychic content and relationship to the inner world.

This book offers an experiential return to our innate selves, our inner space. A place that honors dreams in their multiplicity of truths, complex patterns, imago masterpieces, and diverse dimensional revelatory power. It is revolutionary to pay attention to your dreams because your dream space is your own: it is a space that the white supremacist, heteronormative, ableist, capitalist, patriarchy cannot touch.

CHAPTER ONE

INTRODUCTION

We live ecstatic, atemporal, and multidimensional lives. Every night, we cross an especially liminal threshold into the wondrous world of slumber. During sleep, psyche unveils a vivid, visual gift: the enlivened and animated painting of the dream.

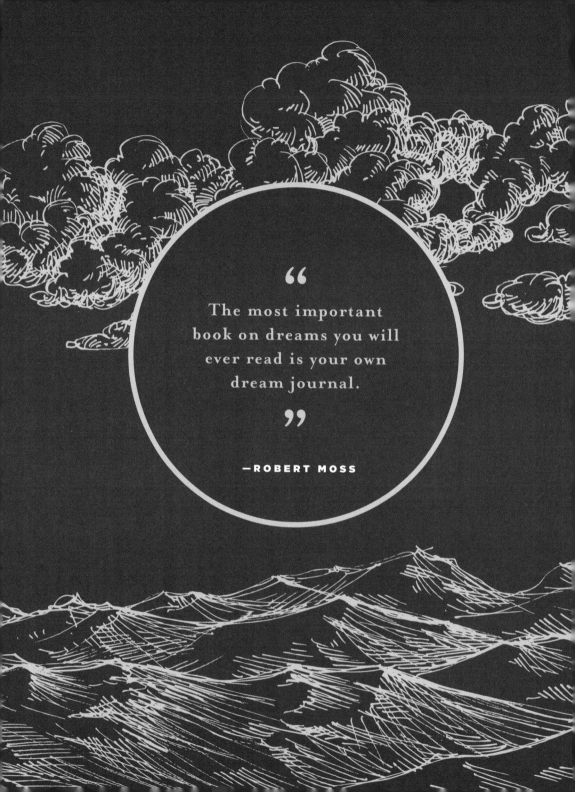

> "
> The most important
> book on dreams you will
> ever read is your own
> dream journal.
> "
>
> —ROBERT MOSS

These presents are some of the most powerful treasures of our creative mind. They inspire inner exploration, growth, and embracing of the irrational. They can act as doorways leading to deeply personal and transpersonal aspects of consciousness. Dreams are generally defined as ideas, emotions, sensations, and visualizations that occur in the mind during sleep, usually involuntarily. Dreaming is a nonordinary state of consciousness where the conscious mind directly faces the unconscious mind. In fact, the most consistent, available, and creative nonordinary state of consciousness humans experience is that of the dream. We actually have a need to dream; if we deprive ourselves of sleep, we will eventually begin to hallucinate—bringing the dreams directly into our waking experience. This means that dreams grant us access to immense wisdom both within our own psychic structures and beyond, into the astral and subtle realms. Dreams are elaborately dressed images and symbols packed with potent psychic energy that express the deeper aspects of our complex personalities and experiences. Learning to perceive these vivid visual gifts as beautiful imaginal metaphors full of pertinent information enables us to access our unconscious mind and begin to integrate its wisdom consciously.

Did you know that every single person dreams? There are of course a few exceptions, such as those ingesting psychotropic drugs or pharmaceutical medications that prevent their brain from producing the necessary chemicals and suppress their ability to go into the rapid eye movement (REM) state. Humans dream every single night. REM sleep is the sleep cycle where most vivid and memorable dreams take place. Moreover, often our brains are more active during dreams than even waking consciousness! According to the father of sleep medicine, Dr. William Dement, humans typically have four or five periods of dreaming per night. Most people who dream experience on average four to six dreams, which you may find hard to believe if you do not find yourself remembering your dreams. But, nevertheless, those fantastical gifts of full-spectrum dreaming experience are there, even if we don't remember any or all of those dreams.

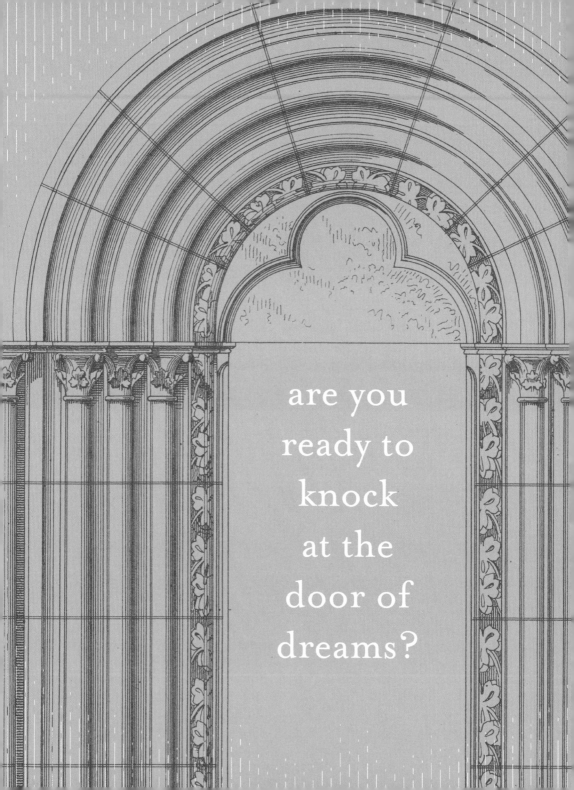

are you ready to knock at the door of dreams?

a dream is a doorway, a portal to remembering the Self. Think of a dream, any dream, that holds energy and feelings impressed upon your memory. This dream can be your door.

In opening this dream, you can step through the threshold into inner space. This dream is a place beyond our limited timeline that expands into fields of possibility beyond conscious comprehension.

Which dream is your door? Open it.

Enter the liminal spaces where the ego loosens its hold. There you can more clearly see the energetic lattice underneath your conscious mind—the nexus of power and images older than human time.

Choice is a powerful tool. Existing in a quantum field of infinite possibilities, we can use choice, focus, and intention to manifest spirit as matter.

Every choice we make closes an infinite number of doors and simultaneously opens an infinite number of doors. At any point we can choose to walk through a new doorway, leading us in a new direction.

Doors have always been a part of my personal cosmology and metaphorical perspective. As a young child I wrote a story with my best friend about an interdimensionally traveling girl who would continually arrive in a cosmic hallway. This hallway was between worlds and filled with infinite doors. Each lesson, adventure, and experience was waiting for her beyond each unique and intricate doorway. What doors are present in your life? Are you ready to open them? Shut them? Walk through to the other side?

You are probably familiar with the egoic waking mind, which we will discuss in more detail later. Generally, the egoic aspect of the psyche is only fully online and operational in the waking state and thus loses its footing as we fall into sleep. As the organic masterpieces of our mind's eye, dreams are natural works of art waiting to blossom into the material realm. Through the process of making art, the boundaries of the ego are also able to dissolve. This makes art a remarkable tool for accessing and setting free the unconscious mind in our waking experience. Connecting the expressive arts with dreams through our physical body creates a space for the burgeoning prowess of the irrational. Dream consciousness is a vital part of being human and a wellspring for psychological integration, transformation, and wholeness. That is what this journal is all about.

I must preface this book by noting that the practice of remembering and working with dreams is a lot of work, to be quite honest, and it is something that you have to set the intention to, and have to specifically desire to, engage with. In my personal experience, simply setting the intention to have a relationship with dreams—and making an effort to do so—elicits a response from them. Just as in most other reciprocal relationships, as you begin to engage with dreams, they will begin to engage with you. I find that dreams come forward as needed, and if you are not paying attention, you might miss precious information.

Dreams are like forgotten messages floating out to sea. The lack of oxygen and attention causes these psychic treasures to eventually sink to the bottom of the ocean: our unconscious. They become lost, preserved intact by the sands of time on the sea's floor. To retrieve these powerful bottled messages, we must dive deeply into the dream world in real time, excavating our unconscious with care and curiosity. Eventually, we will discover the dream's truth and wisdom—a gift, a healing elixir. It is a message in a bottle concocted especially for us by our psyche, offering the most transformative potential.

CHAPTER TWO

REMEMBERING AND RECORDING DREAMS

Now that you have begun to muse upon the magic of dreaming and understand the potential of what dreams might offer, you may be curious about how to begin to cultivate this relationship. So, how do I work with my dreams?

Many traditions have practices of dream incubation. According to the PSI Encyclopedia, "The term 'dream incubation' is drawn from the Greek *enkoimesis*, meaning a dream-like state of induced sleep, and Latin *incubatio*, 'to lie on a kind of bedstead or camp-bed.'" Often incubation rituals are performed before bed for the purpose of connecting with the divine, receiving messages, and psycho-spiritual healing. People would cleanse themselves, fast, pray, wear specific clothing, and petition gods and goddesses to bestow healing or protection through dreams. Scholars Hans Dieter Betz and Christopher Faraone shared the following translation, which is documented in the Greek Magical papyri on fourth-century Papyrus 122: "Make a drawing of Besa on your left hand and enveloping your hand in a strip of black cloth that has been consecrated to Isis, lie down to sleep without speaking a word, even in answer to a question. Wind the remainder of the cloth around your neck. The ink with which you write must be composed of the blood of a cow, the blood of a white dove, fresh frankincense, myrrh, black writing-ink, cinnabar, mulberry juice, rain-water, and the juice of wormwood."

There are many dream spells from the fourth and fifth centuries that share common components, such as using special inks, tying the body with specific cloth, and requesting blessings and divine communication from a god or goddess through dreaming. Scholar Vanessa L. Ochs wrote, "In some cultures, the dreamer went to an ancient temple or holy site, made sacrifices, and actually slept there, hoping to receive dreams that would provide insights, answers, comfort, or healing."

Some dreamers like to write down dream requests or intentions in their journals or on a tiny slip of paper placed beneath their pillows before they sleep. Using dream oil, connecting with dream plant spirit allies, or using a dream pillow can amplify dream incubation and communication. Dream oil is created using specific herbs, blessings, and timing to magnify energies that uplift the propensity of our natural ability to dream and enhance specific types of dreams.

A dream pillow is often handmade with a colored cloth and filled with herbs, crystals, artwork, symbols, or sigils that amplify elements directly correlated with dreaming. These ritual tools can be used to create meaningful processes to foster our relationship with our deep and dreaming psyche.

If you cannot remember your dreams, you are not alone; numerous people struggle with remembering their dreams. This, I believe (as noted earlier), is because this culture (white, Western American culture) has done a very poor job of instilling that dreams are of any importance in our lives. If instead we operated as if our dreamscapes were important and offered us a relationship to essential psychic material, we would all have likely learned dream practices from a very young age. Regardless of your background and introduction to the importance of dreams, now is your chance to begin this practice. Start small: a common way to work with dreams is to record them in a dream journal, such as this one. You can keep a pen and a piece of paper or a book next to your bed, maybe by a lamp or on a nightstand; make it easily accessible. The more convenient it is, the more likely you will be to remember and to make an effort to record your dreams!

First thing in the morning, or even in the middle of the night, when you wake up, just sit and relax into your body for a minute. Keep your eyes closed for just a moment. Then, write or doodle as fast as you can. Simply move your hand, traveling over a scrap of paper or journal—your body remembers your dreams. Just pick the pen up and begin to write. It doesn't even have to look like words. The act of sublimating, or transferring the unconscious information into the motion of your physical body, will get your mind into the habit of imprinting. Do this as much as you can.

Draw, write, or scribble here:

Draw, write, or scribble here:

When you first wake up, and your dreams start to blur, become fuzzy, or dissipate like an ethereal cloud of vapor, remember that the ego does not like that it has no power in the dream realm. Request it to step aside for a few moments, and ask yourself, "Where was I just now?" to invite the dream to arrive more fully. You are calling upon your context-dependent memory, putting yourself back in the frame of mind and situation you were in just moments prior in the dream (this type of memory helps us remember where we put our keys or parked our car). Close your eyes, retrace your steps, and begin to gently focus on anything that arises—feelings, images, shapes, colors, anything that you notice—and bring it calmly into focus. Once you remember something, gradually pull it closer, and likely more and more of the dream will start to come back. If you cannot remember anything, lie there, completely still, with your eyes closed, and just breathe. Even the slightest impression or thought can lead you back into the dream; the most important thing is to relax and let your irrational mind take the wheel.

My Jungian analyst reminded me that even if you don't remember anything, Swiss psychologist Marie-Louise von Franz suggested to write that down. Write down, "I don't remember my dream." Even this small act can prime your consciousness for recall and invite the dreams to begin to surface within your writing hand, body, or experience.

where was i in the moment right before i was here right now?

Dreams are ethereal beings. They dissolve. If you do not pay attention to them or sit with them for a moment, they will just leave your mind. You might even get up to go to the bathroom in the middle of the night, and your whole dream will just completely evaporate from your consciousness. This, I think, is interesting, because it speaks to the notion that if we are not paying attention, dreams will disappear. It is similar to what happens if you don't pay attention to a person or attend to a relationship or feed your pet: they will eventually die or go away. Dreams step forward when we introduce ourselves; when we feed them, relate to them, or care for them like a friend or a member of our family. It can be easy for us to convince ourselves that the dream is completely gone, but they are alive and autonomous forces of consciousness; they live in our memories and bodies, waiting for our honoring and offerings. Dreams come to us because they want to be known; if you pay attention to them or give them any kind of space or time, they will be responsive in the same way that your other relationships are.

Ritual and routine are paramount to our dream practices. If you can commit to five minutes in the morning of quiet reflection and sit with your dream, that will greatly increase your dream's desire to speak with you. This can be difficult, because as soon as you wake up, your waking conscious egoic state comes back online. It does not have any hold on the dream space or the unconscious mind, so the waking ego will often immediately come in and tell you that whatever just happened was not important.

What I find so interesting is that, even after I began my dreamwork practice, almost every morning when I woke up, my ego would say, "Oh, that dream? That dream didn't matter, that dream was totally meaningless. You really want coffee right now. You have stuff to do. Forget about it." I have been doing dreamwork for decades, and this still happens to me. It is a deeply hardwired program. The ego loves to come in and tell us that dreams are not important. When that function comes in especially strong, I find it interesting that if I'm able to override the ego in that moment, the dreams that I usually JUST had were often the most important.

There is this whole wellspring of beautiful and monumentally life-changing information that you have access to through the dream. The work you put in directly impacts the results that you are going to get out. The unconscious mind will generally willingly answer your invitation. If you create an attentive dream practice and you stick to it, your dreams will respond, and they will start working with you and on you. Dreamwork is a beautiful conversation that you can begin to have with the deeper parts of yourself, your psyche, and your soul. If you are ritually creating time and space, dream journals can be a lovely way to track your psycho-spiritual change and growth over time.

So, set the intention and be diligent in your practice to start recording your dreams!

Another way that I like to record dreams is through an audio recorder, or any technological device that allows me to use voice to text, such as email or notes apps. Typing with your fingers can activate a body-memory response that is similar to physically writing. This is extremely useful in the modern technological age. In my personal dream practice, I have used the voice-to-text option on my phone to record many of my dreams in emails to myself. This can be very helpful for making sure to include details of your dream and tracking dreams over time. (I noticed sometimes when writing in my journal, I would exclude details or use shorthand.) The dreams in my email inbox arrive with a simple content search, such as "silver," thus retrieving every silver dream I have ever recorded.

You can open an email draft or blank note before you go to sleep. When you wake up, just barely begin to move, keeping your eyes closed. Slowly acquire your writing utensil or digital instrument and try not to enter fully awake consciousness or move too much. Staying in the same position you were in while asleep can increase the connection between your waking conscious state and the dream you were just having. This has been so useful for me in logging all of my dreams. I wake up and have some kind of recording device ready, and I immediately hit the microphone button without moving my body, keeping my eyes closed as I try to speak clearly while recounting the entire dream picture and my experience of it. I find that I include more information and details, and as I begin to speak the dream aloud, more dream material starts to surface. Even if you start with just one image or sensation or feeling in your body, often the whole dream will come back to you. I call that fishing the dream out—you cast your lure and hook one dream image, and the rest follows.

For example, say you are feeling that it was warm or it was sunny or maybe you remember the slight impression that there was a tree. It could be anything. Gently begin to bring that detail into focus. If you have ever meditated or worked with visualizations or psychic images, this is a similar process. Let it arise and come to you; and then, using your mind, softly bring it into focus. Consider, using curiosity and openness, what did the tree feel like? What kind of tree was it? If you can get more detail, then you may be able to bring back the whole environment that you were in, and then the feelings that you were having, and perhaps even other characters or animals or objects that were there with you in the dream.

If you are using a voice-to-text implement and speaking while this gradual recall is happening, then the dream recall process is simultaneously recorded. Often, I'll get a little something during this process—a feeling, a color—and then I can use it to begin to step backward into my dream. I like to log my dreams by the date and title. It is also helpful to record events that are going on in your waking life during that time (as you will see, I have included space for that in the journal entry pages). A dream journal in conjunction with a waking journal is optimal for self-awareness and psychic growth; it helps to map our emotional life and dreaming life, furthering connections, parallels, and a conscious relationship between the two. Even if you just doodle without writing down the dream, even if you just write down one word, you can always come back to the dream and reexperience it in your body. This is something that is so beautiful about dreams: you can have dreams from a decade ago that will emerge and flood your body as soon as you start to read what you wrote at that time, even if it is just a tiny snippet. This felt sense of the dream opens you to a more direct experience than a simple memory. Memories are often remembered so many times that they start to lose their original impact and truth, which is why written or recorded recollection is so important to honor the dream.

If you are trying to engage with symbols and images in your dream, you can track how those evolve over time and how you interact with them. You may notice them mirroring your experience far into the future, such as predictive dreams that carry elements of our waking life, symbolically, literally, or emotionally; or they might offer reflections on the past, experiences we have long buried or forgotten. Something that is wonderful about dream space is that it is not bound to the same physical and temporal laws as our waking experience. Time in a dream is not necessarily a linear sequence. It could be that the beginning of the dream pertains to the future or to the past. It is not always about our present experience, but yet it might directly apply to our present experience. The dream is giving us information that could be based in the future or come from the past, but either way, we need it right now. Dream consciousness can access past lives in addition to present experiences, as well as the future and other psychic realms. Depending on your beliefs and your personal practice, there is a way to access dreams and work with them in all different types of spiritual, psychological, or religious contexts. The next few pages offer you a space to begin your own practice of documenting and unpacking your dreams!

DREAM TITLE   DATE

Just now I was . . .

_____

_____

_____

_____

_____

_____

What in the dream really attracts you?

_____

_____

_____

What energy or image feels the most magnetic?

_____

_____

_____

Impressions from waking consciousness:

_____

_____

_____

DREAM TITLE   DATE

Just now I was . . .

What in the dream really attracts you?

What energy or image feels the most magnetic?

Impressions from waking consciousness:

DREAM TITLE   DATE
_____   _____

Just now I was . . .
_____
_____
_____
_____
_____
_____
_____

What in the dream really attracts you?
_____
_____
_____

What energy or image feels the most magnetic?
_____
_____
_____

Impressions from waking consciousness:
_____
_____
_____

DREAM TITLE   DATE

Just now I was . . .

What in the dream really attracts you?

What energy or image feels the most magnetic?

Impressions from waking consciousness:

After you write down a dream, reflect on the kind of dream it was. What did it feel like? Feel free to circle or highlight any words or phrases that jump out at you if they feel important. Remember, this is an intuitive process, so try to let your logical mind take a back seat and sense into an expansive notion of what might be "important." Many people struggle or desire to cling to literal interpretation, but this is an artistic and irrational experience of letting the dream itself guide you. What holds the most energy? A color? A figure? An image? How might noticing these elements inform your life? There are inherently different levels of wisdom present in dreams, because they are multilayered experiences. You can look at a dream, and it can inform your waking life in a very simple, direct, and practical way. But simultaneously, it can also be a deep surge of unconscious material that could influence your whole life's direction.

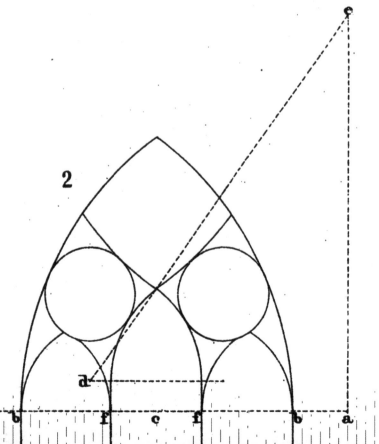

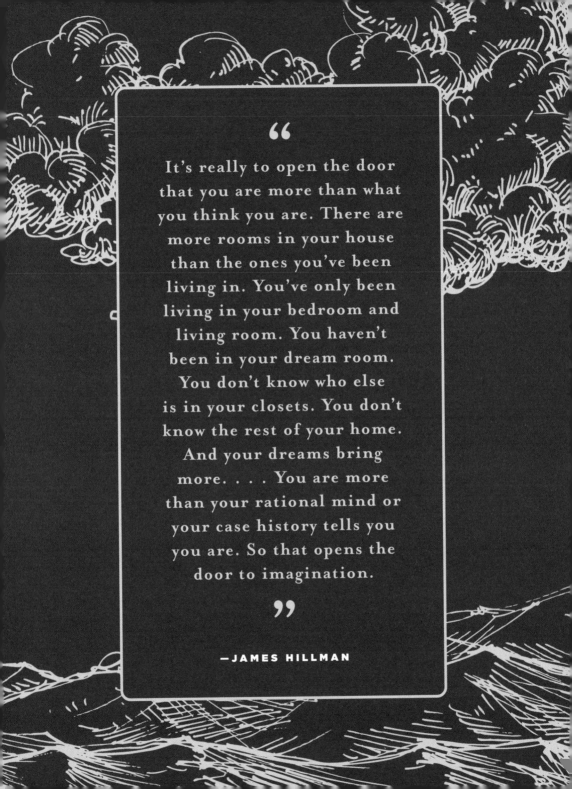

> "
> It's really to open the door
> that you are more than what
> you think you are. There are
> more rooms in your house
> than the ones you've been
> living in. You've only been
> living in your bedroom and
> living room. You haven't
> been in your dream room.
> You don't know who else
> is in your closets. You don't
> know the rest of your home.
> And your dreams bring
> more. . . . You are more
> than your rational mind or
> your case history tells you
> you are. So that opens the
> door to imagination.
> "

—JAMES HILLMAN

CHAPTER THREE

DREAMS ACROSS CULTURES

"Dreaming is a cultural act."

—SHULMAN & STROUMSA

A plethora of theories have been employed to account for the universal experiences we label "dreaming." Many of these theories differ greatly when it comes to the origin and meaning of dreams. However, there is widespread acknowledgment that dreams can be creative and powerful, and can disseminate divine knowledge. Dreams have held a central role in many societies. In some cultures, dreamers use ritual to prepare for receiving an incubated, important, or healing dream. These rituals are well documented in Native American cultures, as well as in Asia, ancient Babylon, Greece, and Rome. Authors Eduardo and Bonnie Duran state, "Dreams have had an important role to all peoples; perhaps this commonality can serve as the thread that we can use in order to sew the tear that has occurred in the psyche of both Western and non-Western peoples."

Oneiromancy is the art of prophetic divination from dreams. It was considered a divine act in many ancient cultures and survives to this day in some living folk traditions. Oneiromancy encompasses the notion that dreams are nightly messages sent to the soul by gods, ancestors, and the deceased. In ancient Greece, Egypt, and Babylonia, oneiromancy was highly regarded and practiced by a specific class of diviners or seers responsible for dream interpretation. Both the Assyrian dream book, Iškar Zaqīqu, and Atra-Hasis, the ancient Mesopotamian cuneiform on clay tablets, document the fortuitous power of dreams.

As early as 5000 BCE, the Babylonians worshipped a goddess of dreams named Mamu and constructed temples in her honor, where they practiced rites and prayed in her name. There is also record of both Assyrian and Babylonian books for interpreting dreams, which Jungian analyst Anthony Stevens noted were "found at Nineveh in the library of the Assyrian king Ashurbanipal, who reigned between 669 and 626 BC." Babylonians viewed dreams as messages from beings beyond the veil and communications from the gods, spirits, and the dead. Assyrians regarded dreams as powerful omens and used them to divine action and guidance. Many of their interpretations were contextual, but some of them we might still find relevant today, such as that a dream of drinking water would symbolize a long life, while a dream of drinking wine would mean a short one.

Ancient Egyptians were experts in dream interpretation. They used healing temples, or sanctuaries, to cure people of various medical problems, particularly psychological problems. These healing temples were called "Sleep, or Dream, Incubation Temples." We see sleep temples across time and traditions that were built specifically for dream incubation and open to everyone who believed in the honorary temple gods. Many gods and goddesses were related to, prayed to, and petitioned through dreams in the Egyptian pantheon, such as Thoth, Bes, Isis, and the Egyptian god of dreams, Serapis.

As renowned dream expert Robert Moss wrote in his work, The Secret History of Dreaming, "The Egyptians believed that we truly open our eyes within dreams." Egyptians believed that we journey through dreams and can travel as far as ancient stars, which they thought to be "the source of higher consciousness, the destination of advanced souls after death, and the home of higher beings who took a close interest in earth matters." Moss notes that the Egyptian "word for dream, rswt, comes from the root word meaning 'to be awake.'" One of the earliest written texts still in existence is the Egyptian dream book, which was found near the Valley of the Kings. It is preserved in the form of a papyrus document with a hieratic script, a type of cursive writing made of abridged hieroglyphics primarily utilized by priests, and currently lives in the British Museum in London (as many of these ancient artifacts do—I hope to see them one day!). This text dates back to about 1220 BCE and details 108 dreams! Throughout the book, the dreams are categorized by their interpretations. Each page of the papyrus begins with a vertical column of signs that translates approximately to "If a person sees themself in a dream."

Ancient Egyptians believed that their gods and goddesses could show themselves through dreams; for them, dreams served as a window into the other world. As early as 168 BCE, a priest named Hor had a dream that he shared with the head of the pharaoh's cavalry. He shared that he dreamed that the goddess Isis and the god Thoth were walking across the sea. In the dream, Isis said, "Alexandria is secure against the enemy." This dream foretold the Antiochos withdrawal from the war, which spared Alexandria. In ancient Egypt, it was customary when a person felt anxious or uneasy, to sleep in a temple where they could dream. Upon waking, the temple's caretaker, or "The Master of the Secret Things," would interpret the distressed person's dreams. Many of these dreams were considered messages from the gods and goddesses for the individual's personal healing, which often benefited the collective. These dreams were considered sacred and meaningful and could only be interpreted by a special, often religious, figure.

Around the eighth century BCE, the Greek and Roman dreamworld rose to the surface of consciousness. In Greek mythology, Hypnos is known as the God of Sleep, and he chose three of his sons to rule the realm of dreams: Phantasos, who brings dreams of inanimate objects, Phobetor, who sends impressions of animals, and Morpheus, the God of Dreams, who is usually portrayed with wings and can conjure dreams of all kinds. Dreams preoccupied the Greek and Roman world in antiquity and therefore had a prominent role in the social, philosophical, religious, historical, and political life of those times. They were considered omens and prophetic signs of future events in private and public life, and that was particularly accentuated when elements of the actions which took place within the plot of dreams were associated directly or indirectly with real events. It was considered important to use dreams in divination, which helped the growth of their folklore beliefs. In the Greco-Roman period, the primary deities were Hathor, Serapis, Isis, and Imhotep who was deified in 526 BCE and equated with Asclepius, the Greek god of medicine. Sleep temples were well known as centers of great healing, or sanatoriums (large therapeutic centers during the Greco-Roman period, which were attached to temples). Authors Engy El-Kilany and Islam Elgammal wrote, "[These sanatoriums] were dedicated to the healing god Asclepius, who took over the role of Imhotep. Temples have been found in Saqqara, Dendera, Abydous, Edfu, and Philae."

The Greek Oracle of Delphi, an advisory assemblage of mystics and a famous priestess, the Pythia, would channel prophecies through dreams and visions, transmitting the words of the god Apollo. The temples of Asclepius in Greece were places where individuals could go to initiate their dreams in order to aid in psychic healing. Jungian analyst Dr. Lionel Corbett discussed the burgeoning religious impulse in the context of psychotherapy:

> Early theurgic healing cults, such as the Aesculapian religion, contained the archetypal essence of truly healing procedures. They accepted the intention of the divine underlying the illness, and their rites tried to establish a proper attitude to it. Invocation, pilgrimage, purification, incubation and sacrifice were all constituents of their attempts to heal. The temple attendants, or therapists as they were called, helped interpret the divine message as revealed in the incubant's dream.

He noted how modern depth psychotherapy practices mirror these powerful ancient traditions. Dreams were considered to be oracular and prophetic in nature. In fifth-century BCE Greece, a new perspective was conceived when the philosopher Heraclitus suggested that a person's dream was a creation of their own mind. This proposition was antithetical to the cultural assumption at that time, which oriented dreams as manifestations of external influences and spirit communication. The question became, "Are dreams direct messages from the gods, or worlds created from within ourselves?" Aristotle even hypothesized that dreams might be premonitions of an illness coming from inside the body and trying to communicate to the psyche.

In approximately 100 CE, Greek philosopher Artemidorus published the *Oneirocritica* (*Interpretation of Dreams*). Artemidorus emphasized the ability of dreams to depict and predict future events. He also highlighted the importance of personal understanding and contemplation of the dream's meaning. As the designated messenger of the gods, the Greek god Hermes used his caduceus (the infamous staff with parallel winged snakes coiling up a central rod, now adopted as a universal medical emblem) to transmit wisdom through the sacred language of the dream. His "caduceus possessed magical powers over dreams, waking, and sleep. Placing it gently upon the eyes of the deceased, Hermes accompanied the souls of the dead to the Underworld."

Many ancient cultures in Southern Asia considered dreams to be synchronized expressions of the divine and therefore saw them as one of the "most reliable sources of insight into the reality of the universe," according to American Indologist Wendy Doniger. Japanese traditions often regarded dreams as direct visitations from ancestors or spirits and considered them powerful messengers to aid in self-development and healing. Dreams are present in many of Japan's mythos, and dream stories depict no delineation between self and other, humans and nature, or the dream itself and reality. In Japanese culture, the first dream of the new year is called *Hatsuyume*, and it is considered to be lucky as well as predictive, hinting at events that may arrive throughout the coming year. Some Chinese beliefs include dream space as an entirely separate dimension where the spirit travels during sleep. They often might worry that if one were spontaneously awakened, the spirit may not have time to return to the body and would become trapped in the world of dreams.

Australian aborigines thought that spiritual forces arose to create the Dreamtime. In the aboriginal Dreamtime creation myth, Wagyl, the rainbow serpent, dreamed the world into being. In the Dreamtime, the earth was sleeping. In this deep slumber nothing grew or even made a single movement—all was quiet. The rainbow serpent Wagyl awoke from her slumber and rose out of the ground. She traveled across the land, her thick weighty belly carving through the earth, making lakes and riverbeds. When the water rushed in, grass and trees grew, and the animals awoke. The rainbow serpent created the laws of nature, and those who disobeyed were turned into stone. She assigned each human an animal totem, and they respected her as the mother of life. The Dreamtime is a space where visitors and guides collide, interacting through a meaningful social experience that brings wisdom through the dream journey. This is a spiritual and collective place, which also includes personal dimensions of dreaming.

The indigenous Iroquois people in North America would often share a dream at the very beginning of each day. They believed that dreams were direct messages from the depths of self and spirit that could guide both the individual and the greater community. Dreaming was thought of as a form of sight, used to locate favorable environments, food, and resources. The Iroquois believed in "big dreams" that directly impacted the health and survival of the group as well as an individual soul's purpose. They also perceived a person who was not in touch with their dreams as someone who had experienced deep loss or fragmentation of their soul. Some indigenous Native American nations traditionally publicized dream narratives and transformed them into elaborate public rituals. These rituals could then become visionary experiences in service to the whole community. The performed dream story extended out beyond the dreamer in order to heal those in need, while simultaneously the dream's message was also related to the dreamer and applied to their present-day life. Dreams were used for divination and it was believed that it was of great importance to observe every single dream. From Sonora, Mexico all the way up through Colorado, southwest Wyoming, and southeast Oregon, there is a rich legacy of what are described as dream songs. The peoples of these areas received songs through dreams that were said to carry the preservations of the universe's ancient inception. For many oral traditions music serves as a form of literature, memory, and a vessel for divine knowledge.

Dreams are a powerful part of Jewish mythos and have been since the compelling sagas of the Hebrew bible. Considered vessels of revelation, the divine was known to communicate through dreams and was interwoven with everyday life. Jungian therapist and priest Morton Kelsey shared psalms that contain passages of "sleeping in a holy place to receive God's inspiration," which was the basic method of incubating dreams. Dream interpretations were deemed sacred. Political figures would consider them in chief decisions and dreams were thought to be symbolic, prophetic, and to contain important messages. Many prophets had powerful dreams that changed the course of history, and the Zohar depicts archangel Gabriel "as the Master of Dreams and as the angel that mentors the soul before birth." Gabriel brings dreams as a piece of each soul's map, place, or destiny in the world of creation. The Talmud contains 217 references to dreams, illustrating their value to mystics dating back to 700 BCE. Dreams led the Jewish people out of slavery in Egypt and repeatedly bestowed divine prophecy upon them. There are many facets and aspects of Jewish dreaming, but one theme that is consistently central is that of death. The practice of necromancy in dreams was considered a feminine practice, and often it was women who spoke to the dead through dreams in biblical times. Kabbalists explain that during sleep, our souls ascend to the divine heavens to replenish their energies while a remnant of our spirit remains housed in the body to keep it alive. They say that we die each night and are born again each day, that dreaming is the liminal and holy space between life and death, a divine portal.

In Islam, there is an Arabic medieval book titled *The Classes of the Dream Interpreters*, which contains the biographies of 7,500 human beings who were said to be reputable dream interpreters. They believed that the inner and outer worlds of truth were directly connected and had a deep reverence for spiritual visions and dreams. Robert Moss noted, "Fundamental to Islam is the understanding that there is a hidden realm where 'true dreams' take place." Sufi mystics describe this hidden realm and its luminous qualities as "the Isthmus of imagination." The prophet Muhammad shared that "dreaming is 1/46 part of prophecy." He would often begin his day by inquiring into others' dreams for interpretation. Dreams were offered to religious and mystic leaders for care, attention, and wisdom; it was customary to be very careful and selective about whom they might share a dream with. Early Arabic practices included sleeping near tombs to invite connection with the deceased, and often Islamic people believed dreaming to be a direct doorway to visitation with the dead. In fact, the "Book of Dreams" holds approximately three hundred dreams depicting experiences of the dead.

In South African culture, dreams are essential tenets of the natives' spiritual processes. As medicinal plant researcher Jean-Francois Sobiecki shares, "In the Nguni worldview, dreams belong to the domain of the ancestors and serve as the medium through which the diviner establishes contact with the ancestors." They often prepare traditional plants to cleanse the body and particularly believe that clearing the lungs by expelling mucus and carbon helps to clear the mind and bring in good luck in order to receive inner visions and revelatory dreams. Ancestral practices run deep, and the living are in respectful and consistent relationship with the dead. Ancestors pass down healing through generations and often guide their descendants through divinatory dreams and omens. Sobiecki writes, "Given the importance of dreams in the diviners' lives, they" create powerful relationships with the land and helpful psychoactive plants, particularly the oneirogenic ubulawu roots, which they utilize in initiatory practices. Like the Nguni, the Xhosa believe that dreams are often eminent communication from the ancestors. Dr. Manton Hirst, an anthropologist and diviner's apprentice in South Africa, noted that, "According to Xhosa oral tradition, the ancestors are conceived as disembodied ghosts (imishologu) in the form of wind or 'spirit' (ngumoya). The nature of the ancestors is well known. They reputedly brood in the eaves and round the threshold and hearth of the homestead (umzi)." The diviner's role was to serve as an intermediary between the physical and spiritual worlds, communicating with the dead and interpreting ancestral messages through dreams and divination to skillfully signify their hidden meaning for religious healing.

While these are just a few examples from around the world, it is clear that, in many cultures, engaging deeply with dreams was, and is still, customary. In some cultures, dreams play a central practical role, while in others they are part of powerful spiritual phenomena or direct communication with the dead and the divine. Dreams across traditions are valued from the levels of the personality to the Self, from the soul to the miraculous and mysterious forces of spirit and spirits. So again, curiously we ask, "Why does wake-centricity dominate the current consciousness paradigm in the modern American west?" That is how you might miss out on prophecies.

"A dream uninterpreted is like a letter unopened . . ."

—THE ZOHAR

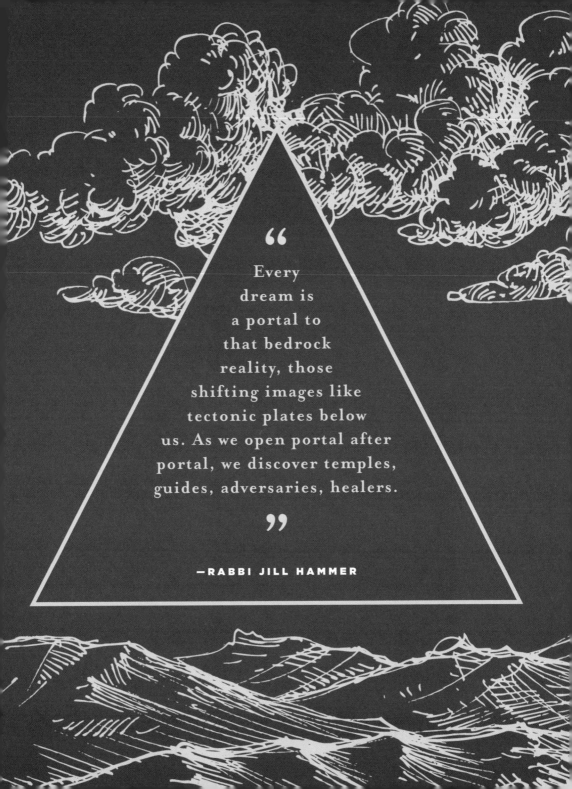

> "
> Every
> dream is
> a portal to
> that bedrock
> reality, those
> shifting images like
> tectonic plates below
> us. As we open portal after
> portal, we discover temples,
> guides, adversaries, healers.
> "

—RABBI JILL HAMMER

dreams are living and evolving myths

Because of the inherent symbolic and metaphorical presentation of dreams, they can be easily likened to movies, theater, and films. They contain costumed figures, heroic journeys, fantastical landscapes, and powerful emotional interactions. It is possible to understand dreams as our own full-length feature films, presented to us as a creative reflection of our psychic processes. As psychologist Eduardo Duran shared, "Since the soul wound occurred at the level of myth and dream, it follows that the therapy or transformation of the wound should also occur at the level of myth and dream." Dreams enact our living mythos.

Dreams are stories, narratives, and even fragmented non-sequitur scenes that can represent our personal mythologies. Mythologist and author Joseph Campbell aptly describes dreams as personal myths, writing that the "Dream is the personalized myth, myth is the depersonalized dream; both myth and dream are symbolic in the same general way of the dynamics of the psyche. But in the dream the forms are quirked by the peculiar troubles of the dreamer, whereas in myth the problems and solutions and are directly valid for all mankind." Each dream has a stage set and cast of characters that is unique to the dreamer, but the emotional content and dynamics are common across human experience.

Campbell shared, "Freud, Jung, and their followers have demonstrated irrefutably that the logic, the heroes, and the deeds of myth survive into modern times. In the absence of an effective general mythology, each of us has a private, unrecognized, rudimentary, yet secretly potent pantheon of dream." Dreams can elucidate the common patterns, narratives, and psychological complexes a person may be experiencing through their own myths in present time. Dreams are the metaphorical mythological language of the soul. What is your personal mythology? Turn your dream into a fairy tale on the next page!

dream fairy tale

Once upon a time, _____went to a(n) _____
                                    (Self)   (Adjective)

sort of _____. It was very _____
                         (Place)   (Adjective)

and _____. They noticed this _____
                    (Adjective)   (Adjective)

feeling creeping over their _____. Looking around,
                                      (Part of the body)

they saw_____that were_____.
                (Plural noun)   (Verb ending in "ing")

This made them feel _____, so they decided to
                               (Feeling/adjective)

_____, into a secret _____. Where
              (Verb)   (Place)

a giant_____ said, "Where are you going?" To which
                   (Noun)

_____ replied, "I am_____
             (Self)   (Verb ending in "ing")

far away from the_____ and am now _____
                    (Noun/ Plural noun)   (Sense perception ending in "ing")

the truth." The_____ began to _____
                 (Noun)   (Verb)

_____ and _____ was revealed.
          (Adverb)   (Noun)

_____ realized that this _____
         (Self)   (Adjective)

journey was only the _____ beginning and that they
                             (Adjective)

would be able to understand their experience more fully, through sublimation using

the expressive arts.

dream plants

Working with and alongside plants has been integral to our human experience and magical traditions across the globe. We are part of nature, constantly rebalancing our relationship to both spirit and the natural world. Have you ever practiced or considered inviting plants or herbs into your dreaming rituals or sleep routine? Tea is a practice that might immediately come to mind. Independent researchers Gianluca Toro and Benjamin Thomas state that "Since ancient times dreams have been important in the life of many traditional populations and the basis not only of spiritual and religious development but also intellectual development, permitting a direct contact with the realm of the supernatural. Dream-inducing plants are considered sacred; they are the source of divinity manifesting in the human body and acting on the mind." We are surrounded by plants. What plants thrive in your environment or in your neighborhood? Inviting in curiosity and connection, we can consciously become a deeper part of our local ecology. Plants are incredibly deep and powerful spirits. We are not alone in this mysterious world of consciousness, and interacting with the ecology of our environment is paramount to our collective healing. Working and cultivating a relationship with plant material has been a core facet of life across cultures and traditions. Here are a few plants that have been known to assist with the world of dreams; many of them simply gathered and placed beneath a pillow can support you to divine nightly dreams. Oneirogen derives from Greek, literally meaning "that which produces dreams." Please talk with a clinically trained herbalist before ingesting these generative friends, through teas, tinctures, flower essences, skin contact with topical oils or blends, or herbal diffusers, to home in on the best-fitting relationship for your unique physiology.

blue lotus

Blue lotus is a richly hued blue flower that emerges from the waters of lakes and ponds. Ancient Egyptians imbibed this sacred plant in ritual, and it even accompanied the dead on their journey to the afterlife. The blue lotus has a vivid, euphoric, and tranquil personality. This plant spirit guide can offer its nervine effects through mild sedation and mood elevation and can calm the waking mind. A powerful oneirogen, it is widely known for its vivification of the dream realm and can help in increasing dream recall.

lavender

Lavender is an incredibly aromatic and aromatherapeutic flowering shrub. Lavender inhalation can help to relax and relieve anxiety and even insomnia. Lavender has been shown to soothe the sympathetic nervous system response, slow down heart rate, and lower blood pressure. Ancient Egyptians used lavender in the mummification of their mighty and noblest dead and funerary process. Lavender's floral scent is calming, eases sleep throughout the night, and reduces nighttime awakenings. It has been known to aid in psychic dreaming, increasing intuition and insight. Lavender promotes peace, rest, and harmony in the home.

mugwort

Mugwort is a wonderful liminal space worker associated with the moon and helps increase psychic sensitivity in addition to the ability to bridge the gap between the world of the living and the space of the dead. Sometimes called "dream plant," this powerful ally can intensify, enhance, and amplify your dreams. In Northern European and medieval lore, to sleep with a bouquet of mugwort is said to bring prophetic dreams and psychic visions. The British Isles called it "dreaming coal." Mugwort has long been used to aid in astral projection and to induce lucid dreams. Mugwort is an incredibly protective plant and has been said to guard sleep from evil spirits and, if contained in a red bag underneath one's pillow, to aid in bringing clairvoyant dreams.

passionflower

It can be easy to become mesmerized by the stunning complexity of this beautiful plant. Its medicine includes inducing sleep and relaxation. It relieves anxiety and is a great assistant for the overwhelmed multitasker. Each of its colorful petals and stamens is neatly organized in an intricate composition, which displays how this flower can help you mirror the multiplex in your own mind, body, and soul. Their calming powers have been used to alleviate insomnia and bring in vivid, pleasant dreams. Passionflowers have sedative and narcotic effects and have been known to increase lucidity and visions. Passionflowers work well with other dream herbs and can even potentiate their dreaming properties.

sweet violet

Well known for their ability to soothe, calm, and cleanse, crowns of violets were used in Greek lore to relieve headaches and insomnia. Their sweet scent can offer serenity, can greatly improve sleep, and can promote pleasant dreams. Greeks would adorn themselves with violets to relax and induce sleep. Violets promote decongestion and have anti-imflammatory effects. These cooling and soothing purple blossoms offer comfort and ease the body into deep and peaceful sleep.

valerian

Valerian is a powerful botanical sleep aid. Its effects include sedation, drowsiness, improved dream recall, and vivid dreams. Valerian reduces stress and is an excellent ally to bring with you to bed. Known to help with insomnia and anxiety, this calming spirit relaxes and brings deep sleep with memorable dreams. Also used to ward off evil, this plant has been used for centuries in healing rituals.

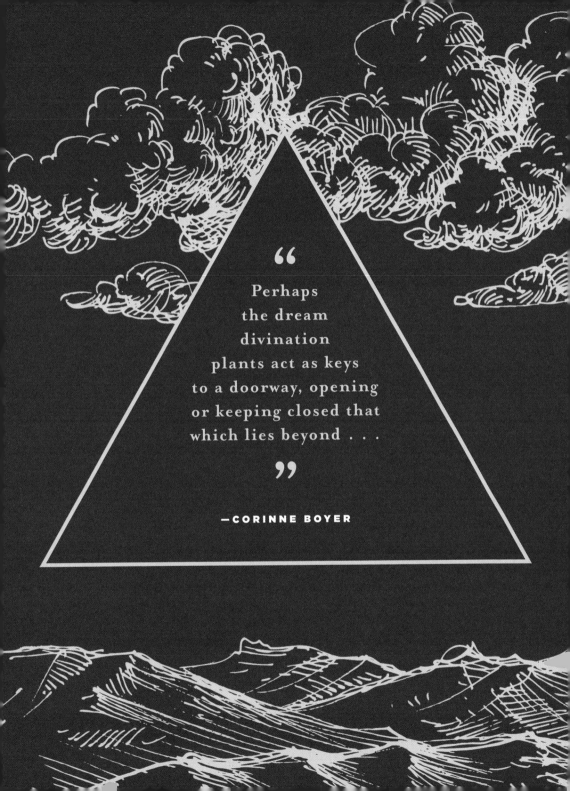

> Perhaps
> the dream
> divination
> plants act as keys
> to a doorway, opening
> or keeping closed that
> which lies beyond . . .

—CORINNE BOYER

CHAPTER FOUR

MODERN HISTORICAL PERSPECTIVES

During sleep, our psyche
unveils a vivid visual gift:
the animated painting
of the dream.

Though people have been engaging in dreamwork since time immemorial, it emerged through the psychoanalytic era as a legitimate psychological way to contact the visual and ineffable realms of psyche within the context of the Western mind. Dream psychology emerged at the turn of the twentieth century when Sigmund Freud began to explore and publish works pertaining to the meaning of dreams in the context of psychoanalysis, particularly in his book The Interpretation of Dreams. Freud viewed dreams as portals to the unconscious mind. He believed that all the psychic material repressed by humans resides in the unconscious and is often expressed through dreams. He noticed that a person's conscious experience was actually a small portion of a person's psychological life and that the conscious mind tended to suppress threatening psychic materials and experiences. Dreams seemed to serve as a bridge to connect with these pushed-away and preconscious states, so Freud attempted to decipher and ascribe meaning to them by studying the symbols they contained and paying attention to their many layers.

Freud distinguished two main types for assigning meaning to the content of a dream: manifest content and latent content. Manifest content is described by Freud as the literal visual sequence or description of the dream (obvious), while latent content is defined as part of the dreamer's unconscious mind, full of hidden meaning (concealed). Freud also believed that dreams were direct expressions of libidinal energy, as well as fantasies that portrayed wish fulfillment. While psychology has since deemed these theories reductive, the introduction of these concepts established dreaming as an avenue for personal and psychotherapeutic self-exploration in the Western world.

Freud supposed that dreams are an interface that mediates between unconsciousness and consciousness. Within the context of society, respectively, he called this the "primal instinctual id" and the "superego," the id being the inner instinctual processes subject to repression, mitigation, or rejection by the superego, the personified aspect of our psychology that is performative, conforming to the needs of the social world and cultural expectations. He felt that dreams could be a psychic adaptation for the ego to make way for repressed and unconscious impulses to come forward and allow them to become present.

Freud was educated in Vienna with a focus in physiochemical and neurological psychoanalysis. He started out with a scientific basis and ended up deviating from rigid thinking; his work was soulful, although not often portrayed as such. Freud intentionally used metaphors, as Austrian psychologist Bruno Bettelheim wrote, "to bridge the rift that exists between the hard facts to which psychoanalysis refers and the imaginative manner in which it explains them." Freud deduced that the unconscious speaks through metaphoric language, which inherently lends itself to a more deeply-felt experience than academic psychoanalytical verbiage. While many of Freud's theories have been mistranslated or are overtly problematic when contextualized in the current paradigm, his work pertaining to dreams was the first of its kind and is still relevant. Using metaphors and symbolic images, dreams communicate parts of the psyche that are completely unconscious, so it is important to work with these aspects of the personality to move toward wholeness and integration.

Analytical psychologist Carl Jung's approach to using dreamwork in clinical practice embraced dreams as avenues into the unconscious and vehicles for psychic transformation. Through a Jungian lens, dreams are elaborately dressed images and symbols packed with potent psychic energy that express the deeper aspects of our complex personalities and experiences. As a psychiatrist, Carl Jung worked professionally with Freud for many years until their differing views on dreams, particularly through analyzing each other's dreams, separated them.

As Jung wrote,

> We were together every day, and analyzed each other's dreams. At the time I had a number of important ones, but Freud could make nothing of them.... Then he said, "But I cannot risk my authority!" At that moment he lost it altogether. That

sentence burned itself into my memory; and in it the end of our relationship was already foreshadowed. Freud was placing personal authority above truth. As I have already said, Freud was able to interpret the dreams I was then having only incompletely or not at all.

Their practice of analyzing dreams both together and with patients had a monumental impact on the use of dreams in psychotherapy. After parting with Freud, Jung's work deepened.

Jung's inspiration to work with dreams in a therapeutic context arose from his own subjective experience. In contrast to Freud, he believed that dreams expressed much deeper and more multifaceted levels of human experience than simply being an outlet for the libido or wish fulfillment. He found that dreams illuminated thoughts, feelings, and conceptions within his own psyche that he was not consciously addressing. Jung explained a particularly informative dream he experienced:

> My dream was giving me the answer. It obviously pointed to the foundations of cultural history—a history of successive layers of consciousness. My dream thus constituted a kind of structural diagram of the human psyche; it postulated something of an all together impersonal nature underlying that psyche ... It was my first inkling of a collective a priori beneath the personal psyche.

This dream contained personal layers but also spoke to an imperative and important aspect of the collective. It was from this dream that Jung first envisioned his conceptions of archetypes and the collective unconscious. In fact, it was during a discussion regarding this dream that Jung realized he would never again be able to work collegially with Freud, which solidified his departure from the school of Freudian psychoanalysis.

While Jung laid a solid dreamwork foundation, many great thinkers and subsequent psychotherapists embellished, accentuated, and expanded upon his theories. Post-Jungian and archetypal psychologist James Hillman affirmed how inextricably linked primal neural and somatic intelligences are to the images that were so important to Jung in his therapeutic practice. Hillman wrote, "Jung's position here states that the fundamental facts of existence are the 'fantasy images' of the psyche. All consciousness depends on these images. Everything else—ideas of the mind, sensations of the body, perceptions of the world around us, beliefs, feelings, hungers—must present themselves as images in order to become experienced." Image as experience becomes the foundational language of psyche, which suggests that working with dream images in therapy would reach the roots of psychic processes for examination and integration.

Founding president of Pacifica Graduate Institute and clinical depth psychologist, Stephen Aizenstat fathered an approach to dreamwork called "dream tending." Aizenstat shared, "Dream Tending is a visionary new paradigm for thinking and living . . . I believe that the DNA of our individual and planetary evolution is coded in the images of dreams." Proliferating dreamwork and psychological perspectives in the twenty-first century is critical to our postmodern evolution and individual and societal well-being, especially during this time of ecological and spiritual crisis. He addresses this at length in his book, *Dream Tending: Awakening the Healing Power of Dreams*. Building upon Joseph Campbell's portrayal of myths, Freud's psychoanalytic tradition, and Jung's depth work with the unconscious, Aizenstat posits that it is possible to imagine a creative intersection which adapts dreamwork for modern times. He discusses what he calls the *world's dream*. This concept goes beyond the personal and collective levels of consciousness noted by previous dream experts and encompasses the "ensouled world" beyond human experience. The *world's dream* invites in the perspective that the world itself is *alive*. Of course this concept is not new to indigenous and earth-based traditions, but its integration into modern psychology could be profoundly healing for the psyches of those raised and indoctrinated in the modern West.

In the pervasive, dominant Western culture, Americans and others have lost touch with this innate expression of life. Aizenstat proclaims, "It is only in the last five hundred years with the rise of empirical science and the gradual transition to urban living that we have lost our primal relationship to nature. I often notice how people today have little awareness of the changes in seasons, the phases of the moon, the ebb and flow of the tides, and other natural cycles." Here he is calling attention to the dominant culture's selective attention. Natural cycles have influenced human behavior for thousands of years, and yet with all of the contemporary technology and intelligence at their disposal, humans are suppressing the wisdom of a consciousness that is much older, larger, and wiser than themselves.

If we take a moment to consider the *world's dream* as a function of what could be described as the *world's psyche*, then we could also imagine the *world's conscious and unconscious mind*. Just as the whole of the human personality and soul is interconnected, so is that of the world's psyche. From this perspective one could conceive that because humans are an expression of the world's consciousness (or unconsciousness), we partially embody the world's archetypes, complexes, and shadow self. This insinuates the collective responsibility we share to bring the repressed aspects of the world's psyche into consciousness. Aizenstat explains succinctly, "Many people came to see themselves not as part of the world, but as masters of it. Science lifted up and nearly deified the supremacy of the human mind—not the mind in its totality, but only its narrow, logical, rational, linear aspects. All of the expressions of the mind—intuition, dreams, emotions, play, and so forth—have been for the most part devalued and marginalized." Dreaming is not only revelatory, it is rebellious.

the structure of the psyche

Here is an illustration of Carl Jung's basic map of the psyche. As you can see, the ego and persona belong to the world of consciousness, the outer world, while the shadow and expressions of our inner masculine and feminine elements rest in the unconscious. The Self with a capital S is the archetype that drives our personal individuation process. It speaks to us through events, dreams, feelings, and sudden epiphanies. I love this diagram because it shows how the ego is but a small function within the rest of our totality; it is vital and valuable but it does not always need to be running the show. There is an important distinction within the concept of the ego: the dimension of the ego that spiritual traditions seek to destroy, deflate, or disintegrate, and the foundational psychic element of the ego that enables us to hold and integrate spiritual experiences. Without ego strength, our psyche could more easily fracture and get lost in the etheric abyss, which might be experienced as a psychotic break.

Jung described the "successive layers of consciousness" that comprise the human experience, psyche, and personality. These layers can be imagined as striations of light through a prism, filtering the human psyche through its constellations and refractions. Jung discussed his map of the psyche as a whole system containing individual parts with distinctive functions, such as the ego, the Self, and the personal unconscious. These are a few of the many different aspects of our psychological consciousness.

First, we have our threshold of waking awareness, which is the general waking state that we usually experience life in; this is truly only a small portion of our consciousness. The ego is what we usually identify with as who we are; the ego functions are an integral and intermediary structure in our psyche and sit a step closer to our true capital-S Self than the persona, which is a more surface-level aspect that we use to engage with people in the world. The persona sits at the very outer layer of conscious awareness. I like to think about it as the person you are

MAP OF THE PSYCHE

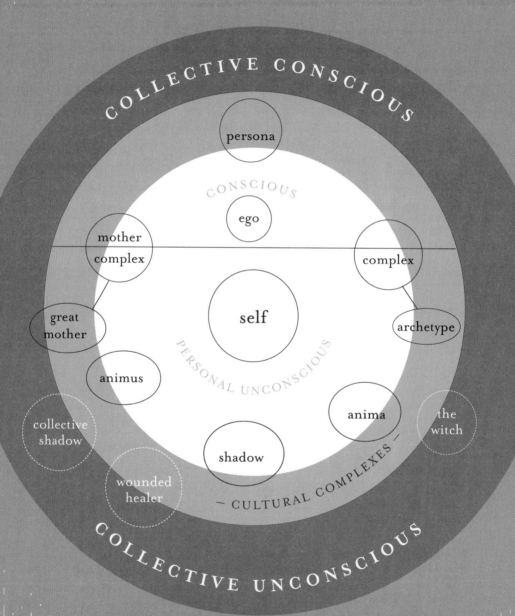

when you go to the coffee shop in the morning. Ask yourself, "What is the first way that you interact with another human being that is natural and spontaneous? What is the part of your personality that shows up that is not deeply personal, just a general interaction or social role that you play?" The persona functions to keep the rest of the psyche under wraps, while it makes efforts toward interfacing with the larger context of interpersonal interactions and relationships. It is useful to negotiate first impressions, whether by being warmly enticing or by throwing up a cold icy barricade.

Waking consciousness's main driver, the ego, is centered in our conscious mind along with its constellation of complexes. According to psychologist Richard Sharf, the "ego refers to the means of organizing the conscious mind. The ego selects those perceptions, thoughts, memories, and feelings that will become conscious." The ego could be described in part as the investment that you have in who you are, the way that you perceive yourself or think about yourself and how you interact with the world. You might think of someone who has a very malnourished ego as having low self-esteem and struggling to manage their emotions. Having a malnourished ego might also present as being uncontrollably flooded with emotions and often feeling dysregulated. Emotional or affective dysregulation has been described as being unable to selectively focus attention, to reinterpret distressing thoughts, and to modulate cognitive and behavioral responses due to struggling with awareness, acceptance, impulse control, emotional clarity, and emotional regulation strategies. From a Jungian perspective this could be because the semipermeable egoic foundation and membrane is underdeveloped: it is so thin or lacking integrity that the unconscious or outer world overwhelms it, almost as if it was submerged in water. A person with a rigid ego might be full of themselves or inflexible because their egoic membrane has not been permeated by the outer world or is too stiff a structure, leaving them well guarded but potentially pervious to an inflated sense of self.

The ego is an incredibly important structure because it helps us psychically flourish in the world. The idea that the ego has taken over our awareness and is dominating our conscious experience is often true in American westernized culture. In America, the dominant cultural narrative teaches us that our primary orientation is toward the development of our ego. This is where we begin to lose conscious touch with other aspects of our personality and our unconsciousness. Our ego-dominated awareness is almost ironic, considering that modern neuroscience confirms how little of our own consciousness we are actually aware of. Dr. David Eagleman, a professor of brain plasticity, stated, "The conscious you, which is the part that flickers to life when you wake up in the morning, is the smallest bit of what's happening in your head. . . . It's like a broom closet in the mansion of the brain." This image suggests our unconscious or nonconscious experience includes the rest of the mansion! As noted earlier, the ego does not like dreams, because it does not have the power to experience them directly. The ego will say, "That wasn't important, you have stuff to do, get up, drink tea," and try to keep you from your dreams. Do not be fooled.

Often concerned with reality and identity, the ego likes to situate itself in the driver's seat of our consciousness. The ego aids us in navigating between our internal subjective and outer experiential worlds. It acts as a stable center, alternately mitigating and integrating information and supporting our ability to adapt, and the individuation process. In essence, Jung's conception of ego is that it "refers to the means of organizing the conscious mind. . . . [It] selects those perceptions, thoughts, memories and feelings that will become conscious." Jung wrote that dreams "are invariably seeking to express something that the ego," as the center of cognizance, "does not know and does not understand." The ego is not an antispiritual construct: it actually can help ground us during spiritual experiences. For example, one of the reasons psychological fragmentation may occur in individuals during psychedelic experiences is due to lack of ego strength. If the ego is not well developed or strong enough to manage the intensity of the experience, the psyche can become flooded and unable to integrate, which can cause splintering.

Living under the influence of Western culture, the issue is not the ego itself, but the self-centered, egomaniacal, and megalomaniacal focus of cultural psychological development. If the ego becomes too inflated and is constantly running the show, much of our personality becomes neglected, and our shadow begins to gain psychic energy. The shadow is a complex of energy in the unconscious, which I will further discuss in the following paragraphs. Again, we do not need to destroy our ego—that, in fact, can be very dangerous. We do need to build a healthy, balanced, and strong ego that does not dominate our experience but aids us in integrating deeper aspects of our Self.

The Self is at the very heart; it is central to the personality and permeates outward, attempting to coalesce all of our layers into a full spectrum, a complete rainbow. In Jung's conceptual model of the personality, the archetype of the Self holds the energy of psychic totality and simultaneously exists at the center of the psyche, but also extends outward into the world. Jung observed the Self as the totality of the psyche, which includes the collective unconscious, and he tended to emphasize the symbolic, archetypal, and numinous aspects of the Self in dreams. The numinous refers to "a dynamic agency or effect independent of the conscious will" and thus is psychologically "associated with experiences of the self." The Self is the part of us that aligns with the individuation process of our lifetime. It is always bringing us closer to who we are meant to be and simultaneously cocreating our fully realized and ever-evolving potential.

Below our threshold of waking awareness is an entire well of unconscious information and material. The unconscious is that which consciousness cannot directly access. The buried aspects of the unconscious may be uniquely personal, or they might be universal. Carl Jung has a quote: "The psychological rule says that when an inner situation is not made conscious, it happens outside, as fate."

By definition the unconscious is not conscious, period. This unknown and almost unknowable mass of experience and information is percolating below the surface of our awareness and comes into our lives without our consciousness, expressing itself without our consent in innumerable and often destructive or compulsive ways. Our conscious mind and ego cannot directly see our unconscious, so we are not aware of how it is always affecting our behavior. We do not have a 360-degree view of ourselves; in fact, perhaps it is more accurate to imagine our view of ourselves and experience as being approximately 20 degrees. Our unconscious comprises around 95 percent of our brain activity! Contemporary cognitive neuroscientists have conducted studies that have revealed that only 5 percent of our cognitive activities (decisions, emotions, actions, behavior) are conscious, whereas the remaining 95 percent arise unconsciously.

As Jung writes in "Symbols and the Interpretation of Dreams":

> All contents of consciousness have been or can become
> subliminal, thus forming part of the psychic sphere which we
> call the unconscious. All urges, impulses, intentions, affects, all
> perceptions and intuitions, all rational and irrational thoughts,
> conclusions, inductions, deductions, premises, etc., as well
> as all categories of feeling, have their subliminal equivalents,
> which may be subject to partial, temporary, or chronic
> unconsciousness.

This is why dreams are extremely valuable and advantageous. Dreams are a clear portal directly into the unconscious mind. The unconscious mind speaks through images and symbols, and these inverted metaphorical strings of visualizations are what a dream is made of. It is this non sequitur montage of emotional experiences, visual experiences, narrative mythos, and visionary creativity that makes up the dream picture, and that is precisely how the unconscious speaks.

So, by beginning a practice of listening to the unconscious, we can bring that unknown information into the threshold of waking awareness. If you sit with the truism that the average person has four to six dreams almost nightly, you can imagine that is quite a lot of unconscious material that you have access to within yourself. I think that one of the most beautiful things about dreamwork is that, when we begin to listen, our soul speaks to us directly every single night. And if we are able to get in touch with that and listen to that, our dreams will tell us everything that we need to know. And, more than that, they will not tell us something that we already know. Every night, we receive a new illumination directly from our unconscious.

The shadow has often been described by Jung as the entirety of the unconscious, and yet also can be localized as a more concentrated area of repressed feelings, images, and energies within the unconscious. By its characterization the shadow cannot be perceived directly, so how do we get in touch with this mysterious aspect of our psyche? We are born completely whole and, throughout our lives via acculturation, indoctrination, and environmental socialization, we begin to disown parts of ourselves and relegate them to the world of shadow. The personal shadow is an aspect of the psyche below the surface of conscious awareness that dwells in the unconscious. It is a complex of energy comprised of all the pieces of us that we refuse to integrate into the conscious personality. These are the refused and unacceptable characteristics that do not go away no matter how much we refute their existence or try to push them out. They begin to fester in the dark corners of our psyche, gathering unconscious energy and becoming a complete, independent, living psychic organism, the shadow.

If the shadow concentrates enough energy, it can erupt through our conscious awareness, possessing our personality and overpowering our ego's will. This state could be expressed as depression, impulsivity, indiscretion, unhealthy rage, or apathy. If we refute our shadow, it accumulates energy and darkness. This can appear as a "black mood," depression, anxiety, psychosomatic illness, or physical unconscious shadow eruptions in our life, such as accidents, fights, financial chaos, and so forth. We see this on the collective level with war, political polarization, fascism, racism, and so on. The unintegrated shadow is dangerous because as it gathers power it can send the whole psyche into upheaval. We are constantly in flux, and this aspect of ourselves is always changing; this means that we need to have a consistent dialogue with our shadow and bring it into our conscious awareness.

We often project our personal shadow on those we interact with around us. Projection has been described as an automatic process where one's own unconscious contents are perceived to be in others. According to Carl Jung, it is "the expulsion of subjective, inaccessible, undigested content of psychic elements into an outer object"; this suggests that projections are extremely personal, unknown aspects of the unconscious which have not been examined or integrated. This shadowy material then becomes psychically disowned and pushed outward, hooking on to an external person or event. By bringing these projections into the light of consciousness, we might consider these attributes completely separately from the person on whom we were projecting them. This process further elucidates how in many ways, we do not see the world as it is, but as we are. Our unconscious material is constantly being projected outward, unbeknownst to us. We force others to hold and carry parts of ourselves that we have not yet faced or integrated, such as our personal shadow. Carl Jung writes, "We always see our own unavowed mistakes in our opponent." You can imagine how dangerous this has become on the collective level. It is exceedingly important that we do our inner work so that we can begin to withdraw our projections. When you have a reaction to someone, it's worth noting what it may be about, noting the shadow. Rather than writing the person off, reflect on your own reaction. What are they doing that bothers me? What is the feeling coming up for myself? Where is it rooted? Who do they remind me of? Taking responsibility for our own feelings and our actions impacts the whole world. Just by taking time to do our individual work with our shadow, the less we project out and become irresponsible about our actions. We can get to know ourselves through our resistances and reactions to people and experiences.

> "If we have identified too closely with the light, have too
> idealized an image of ourselves, then our shadow will surely
> come up and hit us on the backside. The same is true if we
> have identified with our negative side: we could be struck from
> behind by our goodness. Either position is a denial of our
> wholeness." —Marion Woodman

TRY THIS EXERCISE:

Pick someone whom you don't like or get along with. Write in detail about three negative qualities that you see in them and then about three positive qualities you observe that they hold. What is your personal relationship to these attributes? How do you notice them showing up in yourself? How do you notice them showing up in your dreams?

The shadow contains not only our psychic excrement, but also our innermost precious gold. Jungian analyst Liliane Frey-Rohn notes that this dark treasury holds our ego-dystonic (incompatible) elements, childlike infantile parts, immature attitudes, emotional attachments and fixations, and neurotic symptoms, along with our latent talents and gifts. She shares that our shadow "retains contact with the lost depths of the soul, with life and vitality—the superior, the universally human, yes, even the creative can be sensed there." The shadow is not just all the horrible parts of human character; it can also encompass positive attributes. The light shadow is often called the "golden" shadow. The golden shadow can be even more horrifying and difficult to integrate. It contains all the noble, gracious, and wonderful aspects of the personality that we tend to resist. Ignoring our golden shadow can be even more damaging in some ways than ignoring our darkness. This aspect of the psyche can be a treasure that enables us to step into the light of our true calling. Because Western culture has such a disproportionately developed cultural ego, we often can equate these altruistic and honorable parts of ourselves with the grandiosity of the megalomania apparent in Western patriarchal culture. It can be especially hard for marginalized individuals to step into the power of their golden shadow due to the current oppressive paradigm. Sometimes people are shocked or debilitated in a way where they are forced to confront the golden shadow in order to heal and tap into their true nature; this can happen through psychosomatic illness or a startling life event.

The collective shadow is all the material innate to our being as humans that gets disowned or rejected through societal development. Aspects of our more primitive nature, our truly human instincts, get suppressed into the shadow realm by the civilizing process. As I mentioned, the dominant cultural views and paradigm make up the conscious attitude in the collective. This means that these attributes reciprocally have an unconscious collective attitude that lives in the collective shadow. A collective shadow present in Western white American culture that is vital to examine is racism. Racializing is inextricably linked with white supremacist, capitalist, heteronormative, ableist patriarchy, and this dominant system is present within our individual psychology as it is internalized by growing up in America. American psychologist Kenneth Reeves shared, "This individual projection is a microcosm of a larger societal projection, in which groups of people, even nations, dislike other groups." Reeves suggests that the Jungian concepts of the shadow and shadow projection comprise a major psychological source of racism. Jungian psychoanalyst Dr. Edward Whitmont wrote "that racism is a form of shadow projection, in which a dominant segment of society refuses to see a disowned aspect of its own nature, sees it in a racial or cultural minority, then allows harm to befall that minority. Applying this hypothesis to the United States, the dominant White segment of society, unwilling to see something of its shadow side, projects that shadow onto its ethnic minorities, this shadow projection made manifest in racism." We can examine how the process of othering and dualistic thinking contribute to these insidious and harmful ideologies.

Because the shadow is not always negative and serves to compensate for the conscious ideas that are obvious and prevalent, we can see this as an opportunity to gather strength in our ideas, visions, and attitudes that oppose the current dominant system. For example, in our current political climate, we can see the conscious results of our cumulative shadow neglect, and we have the opportunity through personal shadow work to begin to shift this narrative. When we do our personal shadow work, we can then begin to touch into our piece of the collective shadow. In making these repressed expressions of ourselves conscious, the collective shadow is less likely to erupt through the collective conscious paradigm.

The body is also part of the Western psychological shadow. In *Meeting the Shadow: The Hidden Power of the Dark Side of Human Nature* by Connie Zweig and Jeremiah Abrams, they note that "The human body has lived for two thousand years in the shadow of Western culture. Its animal impulses, sexual passion, and decaying nature were banished into the darkness and been filled with taboo by a priesthood that valued only the higher realms of spirit, mind, and rational thought.

With the advent of the scientific age, the body was confirmed to be a mere sack of chemicals, a machine without a soul." The result is that the mind-body split becomes entrenched in the collective psyche. The Western paradigm often values left-brained logic and the striving of the individual ego and belittles the creative right brain, intuition, and our carnal experience.

The impact of this psychic interjection is that the body becomes the shadow. We have guilt and shame around our bodily functions, a mechanistic expectation and lack of spontaneity in our movements, and a chronic struggle with psychosomatic disease. For example, the disowned body appears in our collective shadow through child abuse, addiction, substance abuse, and eating disorders. Even many religious and spiritual traditions reinforce this mind-body split in proposing that the purpose of our human evolution is to transcend the body. This was Jung's finding, too; the human psyche consists of light and dark, masculine and feminine, and countless other syzygies that coexist in a fluctuating state of psychic attention. He felt that overvaluing or overdeveloping any single aspect of the psyche is dangerously one-sided and often resulted in physical illness, neurosis, and psychosis. Jung recommended we confront the opposites within ourselves by consciously confronting the shadow.

The shadow often shows up in our dreams as a person who is of the same gender or age or shares an identity that we hold but expresses those qualities that are opposite us and that we dislike. This theory stems from Jung's work on the theory of the anima and animus and is limiting in that it was conceived within the gender binary. It can be helpful to consider the shadow expressing itself in terms of masculine and feminine energy beyond gender identification. Your shadow will likely be the same energetic signature with which you identify, but will embody personality traits that feel alien or opposite to you. For a femme activist, the shadow might present in dreams as a femme fundamentalist or conformist. Consider your dream figures and feel what resonates for you. Loving oneself in totality, to include these parts of our psyche that we detest, is extremely difficult.

Loving the shadow begins with carrying it, holding it, and making it conscious. Once we begin to own our projections and hold space for the ugly, negative, difficult qualities we possess, we can begin to see their wisdom and become wholly human. Frey-Rohn explains:

> Through shadow-work, a term we coined to refer to the continuing effort to develop a creative relationship with the shadow, we can: achieve a more genuine self-acceptance, based on a more complete knowledge of who we are; defuse the negative emotions that erupt unexpectedly in our daily lives; feel more free of the guilt and shame associated with our negative feelings and actions; recognize the projections that color our opinion of others; heal our relationships through more honest self-examination and direct communication; and use the creative imagination via dreams, drawing, writing, and rituals to own the disowned self.

Using symbolic ritual to honor our shadow speaks directly to our unconscious in its own language. This enables us to create real psychic shifts through even small symbolic ritual acts.

Shadow elements of dreams:

_____

_____

_____

_____

_____

_____

_____

_____

_____

_____

Dream shadow:

_____

_____

_____

_____

_____

_____

_____

_____

_____

_____

Who are you in your dreams? What characters or roles do you play? How do you look? Notice how you show up in your dreams over time; how you act or behave; what you do, wear, or avoid. Understanding elements of our unconscious relationship to our own ego can help us zero in on issues we are struggling with and respond differently in waking life. Our dreams also show us wonderful parts of ourselves that we may be afraid of or suppress so that we can gently meet those parts and bring them forward.

In Jung's conceptualization, there are inner feminine and masculine arche-types that both compensate for and complement our outer expressions. Jung often found himself arguing with an inner feminine voice, his anima, and she told him that his work was largely *art* and not *science*, which endlessly frustrated him. His continual dialogue and relationship with her aided his contact with the depths of the psyche and completely transformed him. She is a huge reason why his creative work is still so meaningful today.

In Jungian psychology, the anima archetype speaks to the inner feminine principle and the animus to the inner masculine. According to Jung, the anima and animus are the contrasexual archetypes of the psyche. They are built from feminine and masculine archetypes from the individual experience as well as experiences with parents and collective, social, and cultural images. These inner figures seek to balance out our otherwise possibly one-sided experience of gender or personality expression. We are all both, but sometimes express varying levels of one or the other outwardly at different times. Our inner experience compensates to ensure the balance of our nature, which often is completely unconscious.

When these energies thrive in our unconscious, we tend to project them outward, falling in love with parts of ourselves in other people. Becoming aware of our inner anima/animus figures allows us to bring them into consciousness and integrate them within ourselves. Like the shadow, these archetypes tend to wind up being projected outward, but often the anima or animus is idealized while the shadow is detested. A person looks for the reflection of their anima or animus in a potential mate or partner as in the experience of love at first sight. Ever wonder why you might fall for the same "types" over and over? They may be holding a deeply inner part of yourself for you until you are ready to reclaim it. For example, maybe you always date professional chefs—but repress the part of you that loves to cook or yearns to nourish others. This is a somewhat reductive way to describe such a deep experience, but it can be useful to consider, both literally (cooking), and symbolically (nourishing).

These archetypes may be useful undercurrents to explore in your own unique identity, sexuality, and gender expression. How do these inner figures appear in your life and bring you closer to your own soul? How might you feel connected to these energies or estranged from them? Living within the patriarchy and contemplating the collective psyche's unbalance or one-sidedness, we might consider how, by doing the individual work of honoring the feminine within, we usher her back into the consciousness of the waking world. Jung wrote, "With the archetype of the anima we enter the realm of gods . . . everything the anima touches becomes numinous—unconditional, dangerous, taboo, magical." What does it mean to reclaim our own magic? Or our connection to Mother Earth and the irrational?

Marion Woodman shared, "In Jungian psychology, we speak of this inner feminine as the anima, the Latin word for soul. The tragedy and the danger of a patriarchal society is that too often it suffers the terrible consequences of leaving the feminine soul in both men and women in a repressed and abandoned state. Wherever this happens, the ego, unrefined and undeveloped by intercourse with the inner feminine, functions at a brutal, barbaric level, measuring its strength paradoxically by its power to destroy in the name of an inhuman ideal." She goes on to discuss the patriarchal plague of perfectionism, writing, "Your goal is not perfection (which is a very one-sided attitude toward life) but your unique totality." In inviting the anima into consciousness, we can harness her creative potential and enliven the Eros within, calling us toward the rebalancing of feminine power.

What is your unique totality?

Dreams are not separate.

What anima or animus figures show up in your dreams?

Dreams are a space where the infinite reaches of our true nature resists the grasp of the colonial mind.

Dreams are a place of radical shifts in perspective, and they offer us space to directly face our most painful and pivotal parts.

In dreams we can access the full breadth of our conscious and unconscious experiences; we are not limited by social constraints, egoic fears, or even gravity. We can walk up walls, receive messages from divine star beings, or cannibalize ourselves—symbolic acts of ritual moving beyond the realm of conscious comprehension into the alchemy of direct experience. These metaphorical and artistic bewitching visions offer us a new way of making contact with our experiences and our truest nature.

CHAPTER FIVE

THE DREAMING BRAIN

"What dreaming does is give
us the fluidity to enter other
worlds by destroying our sense
of knowing this world."

—CARLOS CASTANEDA

Dreaming has been largely explored by neuroscientific research over the last century and simultaneously continues to remain shrouded in the mysterious power of the unconscious mind. Looking at the science of dreaming can support sleep hygiene and self-awareness and create an intentional dreaming practice. Rapid eye movement, or REM, sleep was discovered in 1953; this is the phase during the sleep cycle where most vivid and memorable dreams take place. In fact, often our brains are more operational in dreams than even waking consciousness. Our whole brain is active during dreaming.

Every night we go through several different types of sleep, or "sleep stages." Most of our dreams occur during the stage of REM sleep, although we can and do dream during all sleep phases. We have several periods of REM sleep every night, sometimes four or five. As you can see from the diagram below, it takes quite a while for us to enter our first REM period each night, around an hour and a half, and it usually only lasts for a few minutes. However, later on in the night, we have much longer REM periods. Furthermore, if we wake up in the middle of the night and then go back to sleep, we usually enter REM sleep much faster than we did at the start of the night. This means that we fall into dreaming faster and for longer periods of time later on in the night. Our initial dreams tend to appear more like strange thoughts, and those that occur in longer REM periods often have a complex narrative structure accompanied by fantastical visual sequences and stimuli.

Dreaming is still a mystery to modern neuroscience. While researchers continue to make headway in further understanding the biology of sleep, dreaming continues to confound the rational mind. Scientists have concluded that there is indeed a "dream drive" and that the loss of dreaming is considerably harmful to animals. More recently, dreams have been suggested to play a large role in memory replay, storage of memories, and emotional processing. Indeed, neuroscientist Matthew Walker has found that "dreaming is like overnight therapy." Dreaming provides a natural and psychological healing function. Dreams can act as emotional compasses, and having more emotionally charged dreams has been

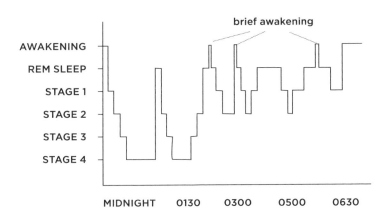

correlated with positive prognoses and recovery from depressed states. Our brain during REM sleep is starved of neuroadrenaline, which triggers anxiety, and this helps us de-escalate emotional reactivity. This might explain why sometimes in dreams we are in a stressful situation yet do not feel anxious. The amygdala is often highly active in dreams, while greater frontal lobe activation has been correlated specifically with lucid dreaming.

Research Professor William Domhoff declared, "Once instigated, dreaming draws on memory schemas, general knowledge, and episodic memories to produce reasonable simulations of the real world." Thus we begin to embark upon an inner journey of imagination, and our dreaming self believes it to be "real" waking perception. We process information in dreams within a mostly closed system. This means that many of our dream experiences involve top-down cognitive processing, and dreaming organizes and expresses experiences that come from within. Aside from lights, sounds, and sensory input that occurs while we are sleeping, much of the dream experience arises from our inner imagination. Dreams are wonderfully creative and enhance our ability to deeply learn and practice while we sleep. Neurophilosopher Erik Hoel explained, "the point of dreams is the dreams themselves, because they provide departures away from the statistically biased input of an animal's daily life, which can assist and therefore increase performance. It may seem paradoxical, but a dream of flying may actually help you keep your balance running." Dreams improve problem solving and support our ability to engage in our lives in new ways.

sleep hygiene

Sleep rituals and hygiene are important for a healthy and robust dreaming practice!

Although dreams have been used for healing across history, current healthcare practitioners rarely ask their patients about their dreams. If sleep hygiene is presented ubiquitously as important, dreams are largely dismissed. However, dreaming actually has a considerable role in both our neurological and mental health. As slow wave sleep decreases and REM sleep increases throughout the night, the paralimbic and limbic systems in the brain become more active before awakening. REM sleep is actually taking place without activating the prefrontal cortex, which means that our dreams are completely disengaged from executive functioning processes. Scientists suggest that dreaming supports memory consolidation and mood regulation and plays a significant role in creativity, which is something I will discuss in more detail later. Research shows that dreaming actually down-regulates our negative feelings by integrating them into our brain's memory systems. It is an imperative digestive process for our life experiences. Abnormal REM sleep has been linked to depression and mood dysregulation.

Did you know less than seven to nine hours of sleep per night starts to starve the brain of glucose? This can cause brain fog, fuzziness, and cognitive impairment. The best sleep environment is cool, dark, and quiet. It should be a sacred space that is for honoring sleep and dreams. If at all possible, do not do work

TIPS FOR SLEEP & NIGHTTIME RITUALS

+ Drink warm herbal tea

+ Take a warm or hot bath

+ Don't drink caffeine later in the day; try stopping before 10 am and see what happens

+ Read a book by candlelight or dim, warm lighting

+ Try gentle stretching or body movement

+ Keep your sleep sanctuary dark and at a cool temperature

+ Go to sleep at the same time every night

+ NO SCREENS (Blue light sends signals directly to the part of the brain responsible for your circadian rhythm and says STAY AWAKE in order to keep your body and mind alert)

+ Engage in mindfulness meditation before bed

+ Limit alcohol (alcohol consumed up to six hours before bed can increase awakening during the second half of the night)

+ Light candles for relaxing, warm, and non-artificial lighting

or engage in other activities in your sleep space. This place should be free from electronics and neon or artificial lights and provide a supportive sleeping throne made of your chosen comfortable assortment of pillows or mattresses, also known as a bed. Carl Jung was rumored to have called the bed "the throne of the soul," and I am partial to that descriptor.

big dreams

Carl Jung pronounced, "Not all dreams are of equal importance. There are 'little' and 'big' dreams"—or we could describe them as "insignificant" and "significant" dreams. He talked about these BIG dreams, which I tend to think of as the redwood trees of the dream forest. But sometimes we have little dreams to fortify the landscape. Jung shared, "Looked at more closely, 'little' dreams are nightly fragments of fantasy that come from the subjective and personal sphere, and their meaning is limited to the affairs of the everyday. That is why such dreams are easily forgotten: their validity is restricted to the day-to-day fluctuations of the psychic balance. Significant dreams, on the other hand, are often remembered for a lifetime and, not infrequently, prove to be the richest jewel in the treasure house of psychic experience." If the unconscious might be imagined as an eternal and fluctuating underground wellspring of emotions, experiences, archetypal images, divine inspiration, archaic alchemical remnants, and shadow material, then dreams may be described as the potion that fountains from this deep inner pressurized aquifer and naturally heals, sustains, and generates life above ground.

What does your dream ecology look like? I would invite you to draw, collage, paint, or describe your dream landscape here. Use your imagination to map out your big and little dreams. Notice, is there a large, forested canopy? A desert with prominent and blooming cacti? A grove?

Draw, collage, paint, or describe your dream landscape here.

Dreams are emotional environments. Notice what feelings are most prominent in your dreams. Notice how your body feels. What emotions arose right when you awoke?

DREAM FEELINGS WHEEL

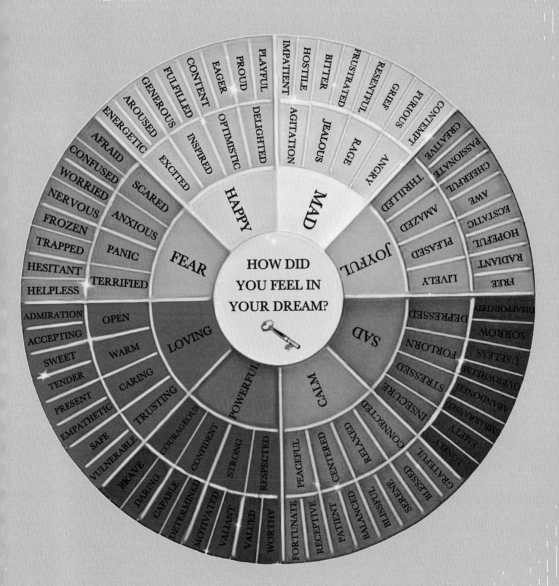

HOW DID YOU FEEL IN YOUR DREAM?

CHAPTER SIX

WORKING WITH YOUR DREAMS

Our unconscious mind is the web connected to everything that we've ever experienced. It is self-referencing, which means that we can follow a circuitous path toward deeper understanding of our psyche's symbolic language through association.

Our unconscious mind is the web connected to everything that we've ever experienced. It is self-referencing, which means that we can follow a circuitous path toward deeper understanding of our psyche's symbolic language through association. When you assign meaning to a distinct image, notice any feelings that come up. That is your association to it: this could be any word, impression, thought, feeling, picture, or memory that arrives in your mind when you contemplate the dream image. Often, you might receive several associations to a single dream image, which allows for you to expand your relationship to what it might be communicating. Each element of the dream that the unconscious presents is intentional. And while dreams include motifs of our collective experiences such as falling, running, and fighting, these have individual connotations for your personal development—so please don't use standardized interpretations to assign meaning to your dreams.

It is important to pay attention to the process of deepening and expanding into a dream image or archetype, as opposed to reducing a dream image to a specific meaning or association. You can gain a more nuanced and personal interpretation by thoroughly attending to both the outer and inner aspects of the psyche in present-moment awareness. This includes exercises that invite information to come forward from beneath the threshold of consciousness, such as beginning with a dream and using personal associations, amplifications, animation, and active imagination to circumambulate its unconscious expression. Jungian analyst, art therapist, and professor Nora Swan-Foster noted that when one remains receptive, unconscious images and material begin to surface and engage with one's consciousness. Then, once an image has emerged, it is important to return to it continually, as opposed to associating away from it, because the core psychic energy is bound up in the image itself, not the associations.

Neuroscience researchers Kurt Gray et al. described free association as a technique used in psychotherapy where the psychologist prompts an image or symbol and then the client responds by describing the thoughts that spontaneously arise.

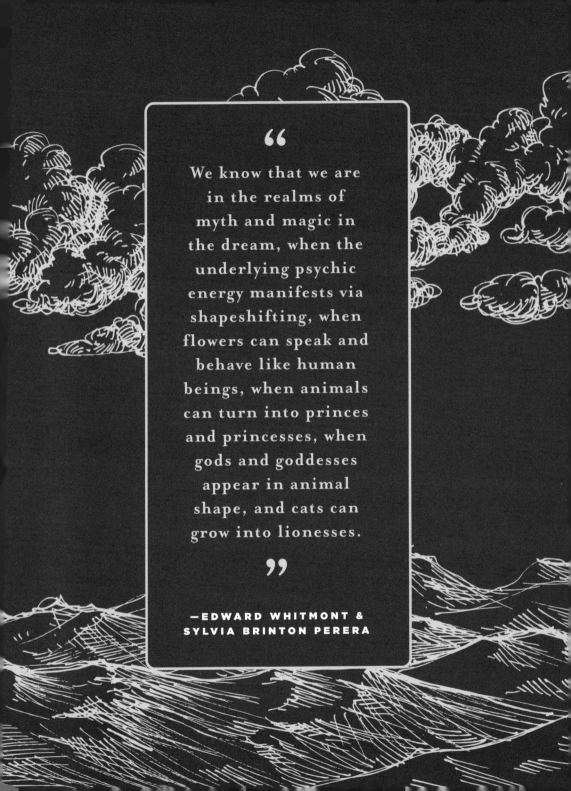

> **"**
>
> We know that we are
> in the realms of
> myth and magic in
> the dream, when the
> underlying psychic
> energy manifests via
> shapeshifting, when
> flowers can speak and
> behave like human
> beings, when animals
> can turn into princes
> and princesses, when
> gods and goddesses
> appear in animal
> shape, and cats can
> grow into lionesses.
>
> **"**

—EDWARD WHITMONT &
SYLVIA BRINTON PERERA

Jung once shared, "I concentrated rather on the actual dream-text as the thing which was intended by the unconscious, and I began to circumambulate the dream itself, never letting it out of my sight, or as one turns an unknown object round and round in one's hands to absorb every detail of it." In other words, you want to stay close to the dream image and continually associate to add dimensionality and deepen your understanding without leaving the image entirely. Swan-Foster observed that by circling the image but continually attending to it, it is possible to begin to tease apart the psychic energy and reveal its opposing and often simultaneous or paradoxical nature.

association

Make a web with a symbol, image, or character from your dream. What does it remind you of? If I was an alien from another universe, how might you describe this figure, object, animal, or color to me? You can include feelings, other images, archetypes, people . . . anything that the image reminds you of. Is the association personal, or does it connect to collective mythological or cultural energy?

ASSOCIATE to the image. Let your mind relax. Ask yourself, what does this lead me to think of? Who does this figure remind me of? Where have I seen or felt this before? Does this energy feel familiar? Or strange? What am I avoiding? What scares me or makes me feel uncomfortable that I relate to this image, object, experience, or person? What magnetizes my mind? First thought, best thought. Try to keep coming back to the image so that you do not associate away from the dream and stray too far from the core energy that is present.

According to Jung, "The most readily accessible expression of unconscious processes is undoubtedly dreams. The dream is, so to speak, a pure product of the unconscious." This concept further reinforces the notion that dream images are an integral aspect of psychological growth. Creating artwork from dreams deeply

DREAM ASSOCIATION GRAPHIC

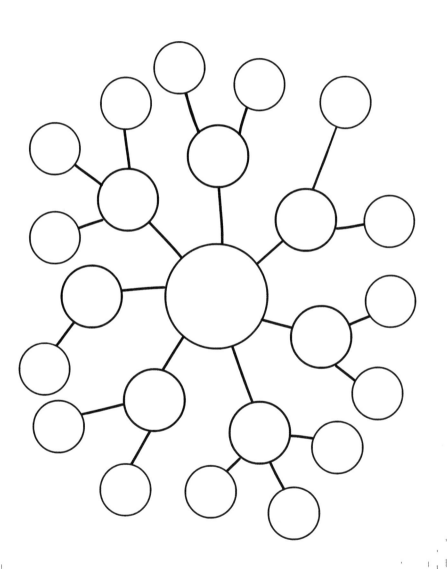

supports the process of individuation. Individuation is the term that Jung used to indicate an individual's continual development of psychological potential. Jung defined individuation as "a process by which individual beings are being formed and differentiated having as its goal the development of the individual personality." This process is the development of the psyche toward wholeness through the intersecting relationships of the self, the ego, and the unconscious mind, expressing a human's greatest capacity to evolve consciousness. Individuation is thus a lifelong path of becoming the personality and achieving full potentiality that one has innately from birth. Educator John Dirkx wrote, "Individuation involves differentiating and becoming aware of the presence of the different selves operating within the total psyche. This requires an imaginative engagement with the unconscious, a working dialogue between ego consciousness and the powerful contents of the unconscious."

Murray Stein, a training analyst at the International School for Analytical Psychology in Zurich, observed that through individuation, a person moves from reacting to the influences of the external world and toward responding to the internal demand from the inner world of the psyche. This process involves a shift from relating to the external world through the persona, which is the aspect of the personality that is adapted to sociocultural expectation, toward differentiating and holding the tension between one's persona and one's developmental potential and authentic values. At every new level of expression, an opportunity arises to observe carefully each opposite that is in tension. With skillful therapeutic treatment, using modalities appropriate for each new expression, consciousness can continue to individuate. Stein aptly wrote, "The new structure that emerges from the inner world of the psyche, in the form of dream images, intuitions, inspirations, remembered ambitions, fantasies and a strong impulse toward personal meaning, gradually destroys and replaces the persona." He explicated the psychological transformation that can occur when an individual begins the journey of paying attention to and working with their inner images.

amplification

Amplification is a process that allows images to arise up through the depths of the collective unconscious and into the conscious psyche on a personal level. It is a specific method where we practice linking our individual dream motifs with ancient mythological material in order to glean meaning and deepen our understanding of the dream's message. Amplifications can come through mythology, movies, books, legends, fairy tales, folklore, or stories passed down through generations. They are traditional associations across broader cultures that reveal archetypal themes. As analysts Edward Whitmont and Sylvia Brinton Perera shared, dream images, "while they often resemble parts of extant (ancient or modern) myths or folk tales, they may also be novel products individually created/discovered to resonate with the underlying life themes played out in the dreamer's psychology." According to Jung, we all "dream the myth onward and give it a modern dress." Allowing these natural connections to form through spontaneous thoughts or in researching the ways that symbols and archetypes show up across history can bring more depth, meaning, and possibility to our dreams. Reading ancient stories and holding in your awareness the present current of collective energies can help you amplify your dream images: Was your dream akin to a biblical tale or more like a modern music video? What are some of the archetypes or myths that might be related to your dream? What characters, story arcs, or dynamics are present that likely resonate with the collective field? Using this technique can *expand* the image or symbol. Depersonalize and de-literalize the dream and find its mythic mirror. What themes are present? In amplifying the image, we enter a larger perspective and engage in the dream's wisdom on a collective level.

What are some of the legends, fairy tales, or collective stories that you notice related to some of your dream's themes? Do not allow your intellect to take over. Ask your mind to step outside the room, and invoke your imagination. Amplification means to increase the volume, so we are trying to expand the depths and resonance of the image and to find connections that deepen our understanding of

DREAM MAP

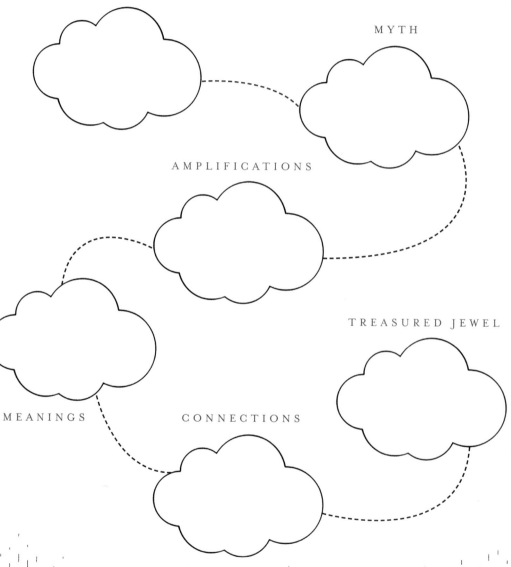

DREAM IMAGE

MYTH

AMPLIFICATIONS

TREASURED JEWEL

MEANINGS

CONNECTIONS

its nuance and complexity. In amplifying an image, the goal is not to pin down its archetypal meaning, but to feed it with additional images that increase its volume and depth to release its richness.

You can look up the history of a symbol, image, or archetype to see how it emerges cross-culturally. For example, if I dreamed of a dove, then I might research the dove and how doves show up in all different cultures. Amplification of the dove symbol might look like relating it to peace or to its collective history as a good omen. In the Hebrew tradition, it's connected with purity and reconciliation, while in Christian lore it's symbolic of the holy trinity and spirit. Looking through different lenses may increase my awareness of potential energies in the dream's communication, but there is always more to explore, and remember not to literalize. You can see and feel into what resonates for you, because although these are deeply symbolic and archetypal energies, this particular symbol was chosen by the personal inner world of your own unconsciousness. So just because you have a dream about, let's say, your teeth falling out, and many people say that means that you are stressed out, that does not necessarily mean that is what it means for you. It could be related to a very personal experience. For this reason, I would caution you and guide you away from using traditional dream interpretation books or online resources—or, as Carl Jung called them, "vulgar little dream books." I will provide a few symbol amplifications in this journal, but I highly suggest that you investigate your own psychic experience to find the true meanings for your personal path. Dream dictionaries are unable to speak to the individual experience that you are having related to your psychic evolution and cultural location.

Always pay attention to what in the dream attracts your most attention; go to where the energy is. If you had a dream and you think, "oh, there was a random king figure in the corner of the room." And then you think, "oh, it's a king, so it should be important," but in reality the psychic energy isn't there for you, then you can feel free to move away from that image. We only have so much time, and especially if you cannot engage the whole dream, just go where the energy is.

Where is the emotional core of your dream? Where's the most impactful image? Dreams are multilayered dimensions of your own psychic map or environment.

You can write or list your waking emotions and experience as you work with the dream, as well as the associations that you have drawn from it. You might consider what actions you can participate in during your waking life that relate to your dream content. This is one of my favorite things to do. For example, if I have a dream that I am eating a chocolate bar, the next day, I will most certainly go get a chocolate bar and eat it. This is a very useful and practical way to show the dream that you are paying attention. Listen, honor what you have seen and heard, and let the dream come forward. Don't take the dream too literally, of course—you don't need to buy a race car if you dream of one—but there are plenty of ways to honor the dream symbols that you have encountered while asleep at night into your waking life.

Use a recent dream to create a dream map. Use your personal waking experience, dream impressions, and amplifications to fill in the blanks. Begin by selecting one dream image; then, see if you can connect it to a well-known story or myth; continue to amplify aspects of the myth that may relate to the dream image. Next, consider what implications or deeper meanings those amplifications might have symbolically. Then, check for connections to your waking life and personal experience; and finally, see if you can unite these threads to reveal a treasured jewel of personal insight communicated through the dream image.

Here is a brief example: Dream image: Pomegranates. Myth: Persephone. Amplifications: Underworld, deep work, marriage, the number 6. Meanings: A season of or commitment to invisible internal work, abduction by or relationship to a masculine element, fertility or birth or death. Connections: Recently I committed to a six-month sabbatical to focus on creative and self work. Treasured Jewel: Be aware of my logic and rational function's tendency to dominate, and find empowerment going inward knowing that birth of something new is on the horizon....

DREAM TITLE   DATE

Just now I was . . .

_____

_____

_____

_____

_____

_____

What in the dream really attracts you?

_____

_____

_____

What energy or image feels the most magnetic?

_____

_____

_____

Impressions from waking consciousness:

_____

_____

_____

DREAM TITLE   DATE
_____   _____

Just now I was . . .
_____
_____
_____
_____
_____
_____

What in the dream really attracts you?
_____
_____
_____

What energy or image feels the most magnetic?
_____
_____
_____

Impressions from waking consciousness:
_____
_____
_____

Dreams can be funny and have a sense of humor. They often include puns or colloquialisms that are contextually bound to our personal environments, generational experiences, and pop culture. For example, I once had a dream about a water bottle underneath my brake pedal while I was driving. Once unpacked, the conjunction of the images presented the idea of water breaking, denoting that I was about to go toward a birthing process. Often dreams will cleverly connect two images to convey a deeper meaning.

Have you had any puns arrive in your dreams? List them below.

archetypes

Archetypes are the energetic undercurrent of our human experience. Exposed through thousands of myths and motifs, they continually arise through our consciousness desiring expression. What exactly are these prehistoric animated forces? Are they gods? How might we bring conscious relationship to these vital and dynamic energies that move on us and through us? As psychotherapist Benjamin Sells writes, "In a word archetypal reminds us that we are always already somewhere in the company of invisibles. Our questions naturally then switch from what why or how . . . to . . . who among the pantheon of the impersonal dominants that archaic peoples called 'gods,' is present?" These deified, personified, and stereotyped invisibles endlessly capture our psyches and imaginations. In examining archetypes through language, from the words of their conceptualist, and through my personal experience, I hope to pique your fascination with these vital and compelling forms.

I am always curious to explore the origin of words and language and how those roots might deepen our relationship to meaning and understanding. The Oxford English Dictionary says the word "archetype" is from the mid-sixteenth century, derived "via Latin from Greek *arkhetupon* 'something moulded first as a model,' from *arkhe-* 'primitive' + *tupos* 'a model,'" and the Online Etymology Dictionary describes the word as "from Greek *arkhetypon* 'pattern, model, figure on a seal,' neuter of adjective *arkhetypos* 'first-moulded,' from *arkhē* 'beginning, origin, first place' (verbal noun of *arkhein* 'to be the first;' see archon)." The Online Etymology Dictionary defines the noun "arch" as a "structure (in a building, bridge, etc.) in the shape of a curve that stands when supported only at the extremities." The word is from c. 1300, "from Old French *arche* 'arch of a bridge, arcade' (12c.), from Latin *arcus* 'a bow.'" Considering the relationship between some of these words, such as model, origin, and bridge, gives us a deeper insight into archetypes and how they might function symbolically in our psychic life.

We find that arches were employed as early as the first century BCE. Built by Romans, the triumphal arch signified a portal or magic door; those crossing the threshold left old selves, memories, and energies behind, emerging on the other side renewed. The arch is both symbolic and archetypal in nature, as it conveys something much deeper than the literal structure itself. In many traditions, marriage takes place under an archway, arbor, or chuppah. This can symbolize the crossing of a threshold, a protective canopy, initiation, and renewal. An archway resembles a bridge and connects two places in one unified shape of a curve. Arches can represent the expansiveness of the sky and moving into a new phase of life. Considering the symbol of the arch in connection to archetypes allows me to understand archetypes as a bridge from the present moment to timeless collective patterns and expressions of energy. An archetype is a bridge between two worlds, connecting the quintessence of the present to the archaic.

In Jung's words, archetypes are:

> numinous, structural elements of the psyche . . . [that] possess a certain autonomy and specific energy which enables them to attract, out of the conscious mind, those contents which are best suited to themselves. The symbols act as transformers, their function being to convert libido from a "lower" into a "higher" form.

And in describing the archetypal content of a dream, Jung noted that it "can so fascinate the dreamer that he is very apt to see in it some kind of illumination, warning, or supernatural help."

Archetypes have existed since the dawn of consciousness. Jung saw dream images and motifs as presenting universal or archetypal human experiences and psychological dynamics in symbolic form. In examining motifs that appeared within his own dreams and across the dreams of his clients from an archeological perspective, Jung found them present in mythologies throughout cultures. This solidified the development of his theories of archetypes and the concept of the collective unconscious. As he described them, archetypes are innate patterns that have existed throughout the history of humankind. These inherited potentials are the psychic impulses conveyed through archaic images that are actualized when they enter consciousness and manifest in behavior. Thus, as Jung theorized, archetypes are autonomous and hidden forms that are transformed once they arise through consciousness and are given a specific expression by individuals and their cultures.

I tend to describe archetypes as a culmination of impressions that make up a deeper substructure of human consciousness, a primordial lattice of eminent energies. Marie-Louise von Franz stated that, "Every archetype is a relatively closed energetic system, the energetic stream of which runs through all aspects of the collective unconscious. An archetypal image is not to be thought of as merely a static image, for it is always at the same time a complete typical process including other images in a specific way. An archetype is a specific psychic impulse, producing its effect like a single ray of radiation, and at the same time a whole magnetic field expanding in all directions. Thus the stream of psychic energy of a 'system,' an archetype, actually runs through all other archetypes as well." You might imagine a single ray of light or sunlight or energy, and at the same time, a whole magnetic field expanding out 360 degrees. If you think about the sun and the way that its rays radiate in all directions at once, the sun would represent the core of the archetype. Then, imagine that there are many suns, all of their rays fanning outward, crossing and intersecting at different points. That is an accurate visual representation of how the archetypes energetically relate to each other. In this vast interconnected web of psychic collective energy, archetypes concentrate at these different points. I imagine this space as a primordial network; matrices of vibratory experiences that hold such a bright, penetrating, and powerful energy that we feel their light emanating through our lives, connecting our daily being to the depths of the collective human soul.

In Jungian analyst Marie-Louise von Franz's book, *The Interpretation of Fairy Tales*, she described archetypes as highly developed elements of the collective unconscious, which history, culture, and personal context shape to represent specific content. She went on to say that archetypes are often expressed through myths and appear in dreams. Von Franz explained that the underlying archetypal forms then emerge as particular motifs more precisely called "archetypal images." She described the collective unconscious as comprising symbols, archetypes, and experiences that span across cultures, religions, and time itself. She saw dreams as a multileveled state of consciousness that calls both personal and archetypal psychic material to manifest through imagery. This concept suggests that examining the way these levels of awareness emerge through the dream picture could be useful in the context of psychotherapy.

Archetypes are commonly expressed through characters, deities, or myths and appear in dreams. In Jungian psychology, archetypes are highly developed elements of the collective unconscious, which history, culture, and personal context shape to represent specific content. For example, the experience of being born lives in the collective unconscious, as well as the experience of a loved one dying and the experience of falling in love. I like to imagine that every time a human being has a human experience, the energy of that experience collects like an evaporated cloud of vapor, condensing in the collective psyche. This energy arises as its own autonomous entity, our collective memory, a group of thought-forms and alike experiences, floating in the cosmic abyss. In this living space, all of the psychic material that we do not consciously process lives on in the collective experience of all humans and continually influences our patterns of existence. The collective unconscious is the ephemeral ground from which our human experiences spring. If you imagine more concentrated areas of energy, more specific vibratory signatures, waves, or types, these are often described as archetypes. These archetypes are figures, concentrated experiences, and manifestations of psychic energy that appear throughout all individual psyches.

Traditional archetypes could be seen as characters. For example, an easy way to understand an archetype could be to invite the archetype of, say, the mother into our awareness. When we think of mother, immediately our consciousness becomes flooded with constellated ideas, emotions, and visualizations that accompany that word or that archetype, and these archetypal figures are not unique to just one individual. There are many variations and iterations of "mother" across human experiences. Going back to Carl Jung's Map of the Psyche (see page 50), we might consider how archetypes work within the psyche. As illustrated, archetypes are at the center of our personal and collective complexes. This means that when the personal psyche develops, it constructs a "mother" complex. This is a psychic structure and pattern that organizes around an archetypal core. This core may be "the great mother" or "the evil stepmother" or so forth, and from that center, the archetypal energy moves up through the collective unconscious ground and into the personal psyche through our complexes.

Complexes orbit archetypes, like electrons surrounding the nucleus of an atom, carrying their own energy and spin. They are made up of a multitude of emotionally charged associations. Many complexes are personal, but there are also familial, social, and cultural complexes. Elements of our experiences, trauma, and cultural conditioning are magnetized to their archetypal core and become frozen. These memories, images, and experiences freeze into a permanent structure: a complex. They can be thought of as subpersonalities, and each has a greater role or agenda within the psychic whole. To be caught in a complex is to be in a state of disassociation where the ego becomes disoriented and confused and the individual may come to possess one of these personalities. Similar to Dissociative Identity Disorder, where the central function of the ego has been disrupted and struggles to bridge the psychic spaces between each part, the identities become fragmented and separate, acting independently of one another. Everyone has multiple personal complexes. Have you ever experienced two parts of yourself that wanted completely different things? Or had an argument in your head between different voices? These might clue you in on your complexes. To the degree that the ego can mitigate and integrate the complexes' psychic energy, a person will not become possessed by them. The goal in balancing different parts of yourself is greater conscious awareness. Consider a time you were triggered and your ego was unable to manage the complex that was activated.

Sometimes I think about archetypes being like black holes: dense, with such an intense gravitational pull that not even light can escape. Their intense magnetic field causes a swirling suction of energy and simultaneously erupts sideways, emitting a bright light. They are incredibly powerful and can also be dangerous—potentially collapsing space and time and siphoning energy into another dimension. Archetypes are the psychic counterpart of instinct. They are inherited potentials that are actualized when they enter consciousness as images or manifest in behavior in our interactions with the outside world.

This brings up the way that archetypes are unconsciously enacted. If you are someone who has mother issues, and the archetype of the mother is really coming through you in a strong and specific way, you can become possessed by a complex of energy that holds that archetype. The archetypes are powerful: they want to be expressed and worked with and have their own psychic life. We can live in harmony with archetypal images, or they can possess us—have you ever been in a fight with a parent or partner, when something comes over you? Gripped by a complex, you act possessed and automatically; depending on how grounded your ego is, you might become fully ridden by an archetypal force—suddenly the "evil stepmother" arrives, and she has taken the wheel. Jung discussed how in this case it is actually the consolidation of the ego that is paramount. When someone is experiencing "psychosis" it can sometimes be an expression of unconscious archetypal possession: for example, someone pronouncing "I am Jesus." Of course, they are not literally Jesus, but that living archetypal figure has erupted and unconsciously possessed them. In developing their ego consciousness, they can better process and integrate the archetypal energy without it taking them over. As previously discussed, the archetypes live at the center of our complexes, and if our ego is not able to mitigate their energy, we become overpowered by these autonomous forces.

There are hundreds of archetypes. The existence of archetypes can be seen throughout artwork, movies, literature, myths, different kinds of motifs, and dreams. Archetypes refer to unclear underlying forms from which emerge images, symbols, and motifs that are then shaped and contextualized into waking experience by history, culture, and your current personal situation. When you are working with a dream, you are working with your own internal landscape. You are working with the way that these archetypal energies show up for you in your own life, which is going to be specific to you as an individual. Every single person is different. You can make a practice of beginning to examine your dreams and see if any of these energies show up.

Here are some introductory examples that I have personally explored from a Jungian perspective. The following archetypes share traits, overlap, and have all had a role in being particularly relevant in developing my personal relationship to my psyche. You will notice lots of similarities as well as subtle differences; these aspects point to how archetypes change based on culture and the nuance of an individual's context and personal expression. Remember, these energies are often embodied through deities; try not to literalize the specific archetype mentioned unless you have a personal and intimate deified relationship to them. I hope the following synthesis will help you contextualize your own experiences with the powerful and universal energies that we call archetypes.

dark mother

In understanding my own psychotherapeutic journey, it was and is important to understand the contextual influences of modern Western American culture. Growing up within a patriarchy, which has suppressed many feminine expressions of the psyche, caused fracturing and shadowing of my own personality's feminine aspects. As soon as I realized that the feminine was subjugated within myself, I began my inner work to discover, celebrate, and integrate a matriar-chal perspective. I realized early in my own therapy that this was a microcosmic example of the monumental task vital to the health and sustainability of the larger culture—to bring the energies of our world back into balance. There are, in fact, many ancient feminine mythological models; they just have been purposely suppressed or erased to ensure patriarchal control. As a femme-bodied person who experienced sexism and misogyny from birth, it has felt paramount for me to explicate and honor goddess traditions through my personal research, praxis, and psychotherapy.

Matriarchal cultures allied with goddess devotion are both ancient and cross-cultural. Lithuanian archaeologist Marija Gimbutas presents her excava-tion of Paleolithic and Neolithic feminine and monstrous Venusian figures as representation of prevalent goddess-oriented cultures from Central Europe to the island of Malta. Researchers have discovered "some one-thousand engravings, reliefs, and sculptures of female images from the Palaeolithic [sic] period have been found, dating from ca. 33,000 to ca. 9,000 B.C." in just the last one hundred years. Gimbutas states that "The majority of scholars have, however, implied that the 'Venuses' have to do with magic, or, more concretely, were imbued with the magical power of fecundity." It may seem obvious that women hold the magical and mysterious power of fertility and creation, but modern patriarchal thinking seems threatened by the power of the female body and feminine experience and therefore has taken great measures to oppress and subordinate it.

Across time, myths, beliefs, and stories of European traditions, the "goddess creatrix" appears. These archetypal feminine images continue to carry the same qualities of life, death, and regeneration. With fertile, seed-like vulvas and preg-nant bellies surrounded by symbols of water, these goddess images communicate the human experience of birth and creation. I have noticed themes of pregnancy, flowers, magic, eggs, and birth appearing in my own dreams across decades.

These symbols constellate to create part of the archetypal feminine mythopoesis. However, these beautiful, life-giving, lush, and nourishing images are just that: they are part of a constellation of qualities that make up the mythos of the divine feminine. The divine feminine also embodies aspects of darkness, death, decay, destruction, and sacrifice. These qualities are not as easily digested by modern culture and are often relegated into the shadows.

Erich Neumann presents an illustrated depiction of the feminine archetypes that includes a few examples of both the positive and the negative, the good and the terrible. The dark or terrible mother has emerged from the primordial depths over and over across cultures, her image found as early as fifteen millennia predating the common era. Psychoanalyst Kathryn Madden wrote, "As an archetype, the Dark Mother represents life, death, earth and sexuality, and deep transformational energy. She has been associated with nurturing, birthing, caring for children, the sick, the elderly, and the dying." There are many iterations and depictions of the dark mother, such as the Black Madonna, Mary Magdalene, and Anatolian, whose images migrate across continents and through language over the last 100,000 years. One goddess whose image has recently been adopted by Western culture, feminism, and modern non-Hindu American spiritual women is that of the goddess Kali Ma. Her name Kali comes from the Sanskrit meaning "she who is black" or "she who is death," translating to black mother.

As Jungian coauthors Marion Woodman and Elinor Dickson write, "The mystery of Kali is that she's perpetually destroying and, at the same time, creating," perpetually in a state of death in service to life. Jungian analyst Silvia Brinton Perera described a pair of goddesses—the dark mother and divine feminine—as "the eldest of fates; Mother Kali and Kali-Durga; the light and the dark side of the moon." Kali and Durga are Hindu goddesses from the pantheon of India. They are said to be the Great Goddess Devi and Shakti in manifest form, "the female embodiment of the absolute and ultimate divine principle out of which all of creation is birthed and consumed." Philosophy professor Vrinda

Dalmiya shared that Kali "is the Primal Mother who brings forth all life even while she signifies Death." She is known as wife and aggressor, bestowing blessings with her right hand and decapitating with her left.

Kali is often shown with her bare foot atop her husband, lord Shiva, standing over dead, decapitated bodies littering cremation grounds. Her eyes are full and wild, blood adorns her naked flesh, and her tongue emphatically protrudes from her mouth. These traditional images viewed out of context by Western minds lead Kali to often be imagined as purely grotesque and violent. Kali's dark mother archetypal image becomes flattened, misrepresented, and pushed into the shadowed psyche. Her posture is active, wearing nothing except a necklace of human skulls and a skirt of appendages—which can be interpreted to represent her destructive nature. Although she is often overlooked as a creative force in favor of her association with destruction, her destructive impulse works in tandem with the process of creation—she is both. Sacrifice, stemming from the word sacred, is a catalyst necessary for creative transformation.

This tension of opposing psychic forces was developed within the context of Western psychology by Jung, which he called the theory of "enantiodromia." He began to understand enantiodromia as a psychological mechanism through his own personal experience, as well as in his sessions with clients. Jung noticed that there tends to be an eruption of unconscious material when the conscious life is dominated by a single-sided predisposition, a compensatory function of opposites. In ignoring the unconscious and repressing shadow material, it begins to accumulate, often resulting in outbursts in which the conscious mind becomes possessed by the unconscious. This notion has been exceptionally relevant to my own psychological evolution and is, I believe, integral for the culture's development at large. If historically within the Western culture complex the dark mother archetype has been portrayed as purely destructive, then her expression as the creative goddess—the one who has the ability to cut through our delusions, usher us through the terrifying birth portal of transformation, and continually generates our innate wildness, power, and creativity—has been repressed.

An important thing to consider here is the appropriation and amalgamation of "the dark" goddess or mother. Much of the literature describes the intrapsychic process of "white spiritual" women, ignoring race and trying to transcend their "white" psyches through integration of the "dark" goddess. While "dark" in this context is not consciously connected to race, it is important to look at cultural complexes and personal identity to more deeply connect with the arrival of an archetype through dreams. Localizing the archetype within our own intersectional or ancestral identities can be an important process that leads to deeper levels of revelation and awareness along our psychological and spiritual journey. Archetypes and deities are much bigger than our personal experience, but it is important that we relate to them from where we are uniquely located. Depending on our personal background and location, the appearance of these energies might be interpreted differently. Just because we dream of a deity does not mean that we are supposed to work with them. They might be pointing toward something else in our psychic awareness that we are missing entirely. For me, as a white Ashkenazi Jewish woman with ancestry traced back to Eastern Europe, Russia, Germany, and Greece, it felt important to honor and engage with another incarnation of the dark mother archetype.

The dark mother is connected to the dominated and suppressed aspects of "lunar" consciousness, which led me to Hekate who is also depicted on Neumann's illustration as orbiting the terrible mother. Hekate is a goddess found in ancient Greek mythology with many cross-cultural depictions, influences, and representations. In some lore, Hekate represents the archetype of the mother moon goddess, mistress of corpses, gatekeeper of the crossroads, and keeper of the keys. She is often described as a "triple moon goddess connected with the dark aspect of the lunar disk." Aphrodite was said to be connected to the bright moon and Hekate, the dark moon. Hekate was sometimes called "Hekate the three headed" and described as the moon goddess.

Cloaked by the night, Hekate's devoted stewards haunted road intersections, gravesites, and grounds dappled with fresh blood. As esoteric author Adam McLean writes, "Her name means the distanced or remote one, and she was seen as the protectress of remote places, a guardian of roads and byways, and her triple nature made her especially present where three roads converged." Hekate was a purveyor of dreams and thought to be a bringer of nocturnal visions and protector from night terrors, which aligns with her depiction as the queen of the underworld presiding over the dark recesses of our unconsciousness. Ruling over departed souls as high priestess of the occult, she was said to wander with those disembodied, her appearance marked by dogs howling.

Hekate embodies the dark face of the dark new moon and according to Greek mythology was given dominion over the sky, the earth, and the underworld, akin to birth, life, and death. Because of the emergence of patriarchy, dualism ensured that lunar and solar consciousness were perceived as opposing forces. This led the Western psyche to associate Hekate with evil, negativity, and even devil worship. Her image was distorted by the projections of the dominant Christian culture, while she became widely known as the goddess, queen, and mother of the witches. Also sometimes called the "queen of ghosts," medieval inhabitants reported visions of witches flying through the air with Hekate at their helm, leading ghostly figures across the night sky.

the witch

The witch emerged from the womb of the great mother archetype and has captured imaginations for centuries. Often a feminine figure, she embodies the magic of a spellcaster, connected with the darkness of night and often death. The witch holds healing powers connected to the natural world, cycles of the moon, and sovereignty. She often is outcasted or imbued with qualities of the outsider. Witches often hold the crude darkness, malevolence, and rejected nature of feminine power. Witches are nonconformist beings and don't adhere to social constructs, such as the patriarchal expectations to nurture men or children.

In her dissertation, *What the Witch Knows: A Hermeneutic Depth Psychological Examination of the Salem Trials*, Dr. Heidi Mezzatesta explained, "With the rise of monotheistic religion and the evolution of patriarchal cultural consciousness, the witch became the symbol of the dark side of the feminine." The witch has been forced to carry cultural projections, often functioning as a scapegoat for psychological or spiritual shadow material during tense historical transitions. Witches held the abhorrent, denied, and repressed aspects of puritanical religious dogma and societal norms; the wild feminine was rejected, villainized, and outcast. As author and professor Dr. Serinity Young states, "Ideas about witches became entangled with Christian notions of evil, the devil, sexuality, and women to such a remarkable degree that Christianity faced the problem of distinguishing itself from witchcraft." These split-off aspects of the abject feminine gather power in the recesses of our collective consciousness and arise as devouring, aggressive, and hostile.

The witch: outlawed by patriarchal society, she is full of powerful spells and secret knowledge—her connection to Self, nature, and spirit is resilient and uncompromising. The witch is connected to her sovereignty, to the earth, to flesh and blood. She holds us at the precipice of the underworld. Jungian Ann Ulanov explored the archetype of the witch in detail, sharing, "The witch figure presents an awesome image of the primordial feminine—concerned with herself. Maternal life spends itself like life's blood flowing outward to nourish the souls and bodies of loved ones. In the witch figure, life flows inward and downward to feed the dark recesses of a woman's psyche or a man's anima." Moving away from the consciousness-bearing, earthly-plane power of the mother, the witch plunges energy toward the archetypal dimension. Unlike the dark mother, the witch is

MAP OF THE FEMININE
ADAPTED FROM ERICH NEUMANN

not solely predestined to give, create, or destroy: she feeds herself, sustaining our primordial wildness and bringing energy back down toward the archaic unconscious. There are many great witches depicted throughout cultures and across timelines; these sorceress figures blur the lines of good and evil, holding the power to both heal and harm.

Connected to the archetype of the dark mother, as mentioned, the Greek goddess Hekate is often described as the mother of witches. Hekate has been viewed as the queen of the night, having a deep connection with the unseen, prophetic, and spiritual realms. She is often depicted with dogs or a Cerberus, the three-headed hound belonging to Hades. Hekate is a multidimensional goddess who traverses not only the temporal plane but goes deep into the underworld with her torch of fire to light the way. Her glowing torch can be thought of as underworld consciousness, a light in the darkness. Professor Mark Montijo, Ph.D., describes Hekate as "the goddess of intuitive and psychic wisdom" and goes on to say,

> In betwixt and between liminal space, she sees the connection between past, present and future. At every fork in the road, she recalls the shape of the past, sees the present honestly and with clarity, and has a sense of what lies ahead on a soul level. Psychotherapists can serve as embodiments of Hekate for their clients. Clients are usually at a crossroads when they choose to enter your consult room. The psychotherapist brings that which is in the darkness into the light, that which is unconscious into conscious awareness much like Hekate did for Demeter when she took flaming torches in each hand and guided her in the search for Persephone in the underworld.

This explication of Hekate's role and archetypal presence was particularly illuminating for me as both a practicing witch and psychotherapist. I often encounter clients at a psychological crossroads, bringing a torch of consciousness, together we cross the threshold into the unconscious and begin the labyrinthine journey of following the depths of psyche toward individuation.

The witch archetype is frequently connected to the triptych of maiden, mother, and crone, and the archetypal qualities of the number three, represented often in typical Greek figures of Hekate by three bodies and/or heads. Etymology of the word *witch* comes from the title *hagazussa*, meaning "fence rider." The fence in this case is metaphorical: witches occupy the liminal space between the threshold of life and death—the crossroads. Witches can see into the past, present, and future. Psychologically, the witch may emerge when we need a guide to bring us across the boundary into a new iteration of ourselves. The witch is between worlds, the conscious and the unconscious, and arrives to facilitate our awakening, death, and rebirth. Witches are often thought to inhabit the most remote crevices of the psyche, making them difficult to access. They can hold a vengeful quality and symbolically express a shadow element or image of terror.

As Ulanov noted, they can thrive in the most gruesome and barren places, revitalizing even the darkest recesses of consciousness. The witch holds the mysterious qualities of the gaping abyss. Ulanov writes, "She speaks for the nether world of unseen forces, indefinable purposes [and] brings a sense of an unspeakable dimension into our world of words." The witch bows to the unconscious in that their existence is not ego-centered, relieving them of morals and values and allowing them to cross between sides, perspectives, and visions of beingness. The witch lives in connection to the all: "She constructs within herself living connection to non-personal, unconscious, collective life processes. Her 'work,' concocting spells, mixing potions, elaborating secret formulas, symbolizes our 'work,' improvising personal connection to the awful largeness of being." This is a nonego space, a nonpersonal and collective space, which simultaneously expands us and makes us acutely aware of our own delineation and individual experience. Scholar Kristen Sollée shared that, in a modern context, "being a witch means: the power to boldly

and unapologetically embrace nature, heal yourself, and heal your community."
It also means sacrificing aspects of humanness and "normal" life to enter spaces
others fear to tread, dedicating time and energy to deepen invisible relationships
and to embody spirits from beyond.

The modern witch has emerged to the forefront of modern and popular
culture in new ways and perhaps now more than ever (for example, social media).
The witch insists we invoke her, honor her, and express her. The witch endures,
but how? And why? Psychologist and witch Dr. Cyndi Brannen queries, "With
all the travails of the witch, why then does the archetype persist? Perhaps more
importantly, why is the witch so popular today. The answer is the same for both
questions: she persists because she is anima, the feminine soul of the world."
Often portrayed in connection to the wilding of feminine power, the witch bursts
forth from the irrational, the feral world soul that propels the universe, the anima
mundi. The inner force of the anima cannot be tamed or domesticated, she ever
leads us toward our passionate and ferocious depths, fierce and uncompromising.
Welcoming the witch archetype into one's life allows reconnection to the shadowy
face of our forgotten, subjugated, and powerful inner space. This path is not for
everyone, the witch is othered, feared and relentless. The witch demands respect
and is not to be trifled with.

the wounded healer

Asclepius, a well-known wounded healer archetype in psychology, is often
depicted wielding a snake-entwined staff. Asclepius was the son of Apollo and
a woman named Koronis who Apollo jealously had burned on a funeral pyre.
Not wanting his son to die, he rescued the baby from her burning womb as she
died. Apollo entrusted Chiron to mentor Asclepius in the art of healing, a boy
whose birth was fated with death and who might find seeds of light in the depths
of suffering. Scholar and coauthors Gregory Tsoucalas and George Androutsos
wrote, "He was undeniably the best-known practitioner of medicine in mythology

and was said to be able to resurrect the dead, which reflected his strong chthonic nature, reinforced by iconography depicting him with his steadfast companion, the snake." Through its etymological explication, the name Asclepius itself reveals a deep connection to snakes:

The first part, "Ascl" (Greek: Ασκλ), derives from the word Ascalavo (Greek: Ασκαλαβo), which means snake (Greek: οφις or φιδι), while the second part "epius" (Greek: ηπιoς) means meek or gentle. The Greek word for snake, οφις (ofis), derives from the Greek word ωφθην (ofthin), which means he who sees everything, the guardian.

Asclepius was destined through the bestowing of his name to be a seer, guardian, and gentle snake healer. He was known to hold the power of rejuvenation, like the snake, casting off old skin, which symbolized freeing oneself from illness. He was known to hold the power of rejuvenation, like the snake, casting off old skin, which symbolized freeing oneself from illness. His teacher, Chiron, was a healer in desperate need of healing himself, after being shot by Hercules with poison arrows. This is where the often-described "Chironian wound" comes from, as well as both Asclepius's and Chiron's reputations as wounded healers. You may be familiar with the Chiron placement in your astrological natal chart, which highlights how core wounds play out in the theatrical story of your life. Chiron shows us where we can transform our pain into power.

One of Jung's contemporaries, author Karl Kerényi, wrote that the wounded-healer archetype refers psychologically to the capacity of feeling "at home in the darkness of suffering" in order to purposefully bring forward the illuminating light of Asclepius. Although Asclepius died, he returned to life to continue to heal others. The wounded healer is able to achieve a potential that they were only able to gain access to through their wound. Consider the metaphor of a crack being what lets the light in. This notion highlights that these perceived wounds, faults, or cracks are agents of clarity and brilliance. Jung writes: it is in a person's "own hurt that gives the measure of his power to heal. This and nothing else, is the meaning of the Greek myth of the wounded physician," referring to Asclepius. In considering both the light and shadow aspects of Asclepius, in using his snake's venom he could both inflict poisonous wounds as well as heal them. Jung's colleague Marie-Louise von Franz said, "the wounded healer is the archetype of the Self—one of its most widespread features—and is at the bottom of all genuine healing procedures."

Often along the path of the wounded healer there is a shedding of skin, small deaths that lead to new growth and regeneration. These are, again, themes related to the symbol of the snake medicine that Asclepius holds, which led me to the following dream.

I was in a sort of dark cloud, an ethereal cave. I couldn't see beyond what was ten feet in front of me. I glimpsed an old man; he was wearing a dark hooded cloak, and I could only see his long scraggly white beard, not the details of his face. He clasped a wooden staff. I thought the wood had been carved out and it looked knobby, but upon closer inspection I realized there was a snake entwining his staff. He approached a gate and held the staff up horizontally so that it was parallel with the ground. He began to insert the staff like a key into the gate's lock. I realized in that moment that I was dreaming, and he turned around to face me and said, "You have to ask the snake why some of the spirals are going backwards . . . they are the key."

In this dream the spiral is connected to the snake staff, which is the key. This archetypal image arrives as the energetic underpinning in our universe, from the macrocosmic swirling of galaxies to the microcosmic twist of our DNA. Carl Jung wrote in *Dream Analysis*, "Psychologically you develop in a spiral, you always come over the same point where you have been before, but it is never exactly the same, it is either above or below." The spiral offers us a new vantage point along our life's path; we are never in the same place twice. Although sometimes patterns or spaces might feel too familiar or like a psychological hindrance, the spiral is a reminder that reflection backward is vital to moving forward. In therapy, often we say that regression must precede progression; time and time again we must revisit old wounds before we can heal and forge ahead. As Buddhist and teacher Barry Gillespie notably shared, "The path isn't a straight line; it's a spiral. You continually come back to things you thought you understood and see deeper truths."

The Asclepius archetype may have arrived to me in dreams, initially, to invite me to begin my ancestral healing process so that I can be of better service to others within the context of psychotherapy. Healing and transformation can occur through exploring your unique ancestral story. As wounded healers, part of our story might be that despite ancestral trauma, we choose to transform the pain of our past into the present, the gift of helping others. As a Jewish woman, I carry over a millennium of transgenerational and ancestral trauma, and I know this energy has served a powerful purpose and role in calling me toward a healing profession. In Rabbi and depth psychotherapist Tirzah Firestone's book, Wounds into Wisdom: Healing Intergenerational Jewish Trauma, she begins chapter one by describing a powerful dream she received at age twenty-five. In her dream the lavishly adorned skeletons of her ancestors speak to her and tell her to live a beautiful life, the life they were not able to live. This notion holds the healing potential for many bloodlines that have endured torture, oppression, and incessant suffering; live the life that your ancestors could not, feel the joy and eat the food that they could not, heal them through your experience. Consider how archetypes and mythology might help you connect with and uncover your own psychological stories? How do these energies emerge through your dreams?

Each archetype has different patterns of behavior and nuances of character. The archetype might not show up in its quintessential form. It could be a varied kind of expression or flavor of the archetypal energy. The underlying archetypal forms then emerge as particular motifs and archetypal images. These images describe a much deeper ineffable experience that humans have embodied from time immemorial. Because archetypes themselves are so elusive and impossible to see directly, it is more common to discuss the images through which they are expressed.

Archetypal psychology is alive and active, a simultaneous pluralistic manifestation of the complexity and depth of soul. It embodies the creative action and multiplicity of expressions encompassed within the archetype's illustration. Archetypal Psychologist James Hillman noted that, "To see through the literal image is to glimpse the soul. Imagistic perception is psychological vision. In this sense, archetypal psychology is a redundancy. All psychology based in aesthetics is archetypal." This explains how Hillman has directly linked soul with image. He wrote, "Psychology can tend to the soul when soul is perceived properly through image." Images are humans' innate connection to artistic expression, which is inextricably linked to soul.

A single image is worth a thousand words, so the proverb says, which encompasses a multiplicity of thoughts, feelings, reactions, and interpretations. Hillman's work is about allowing this multiplicity to arise from the depths of the soul, as opposed to constricting human psychology to simple words and definitions. According to Hillman, language used in its proper form limits the experience of our own psychology. He wrote, "words are the very fundamentals of conscious existence, yet they are also severed from things and from truth." Hillman, in his lecture, The Alchemy of Psychology, comments on Jungian psychology and presents the dialectical dichotomy of "instinct versus image," proclaiming, "Images are so important in Jungian therapy. Jung's theory of the image is the instinct, not a substitute for the instinct. You don't have a full instinct if you don't have an image." In this statement, Hillman is reiterating how inextricably linked our primal neural and somatic intelligences are to the archetypal images that were so important to Jung in his therapeutic practice. Hillman affirms, "Images and metaphors present themselves always as living psychic subjects with which I am obliged to be in relation." Invoking these primordial and soulful images in the conscious state facilitates the embodiment of their raw and instinctual energy in the present moment, thus, honoring the true aliveness of this psychic energy and its expression, which allows it to begin to move and transform.

Gods and goddesses live within us. The image of Athena might arise as you take an uncompromising stance on an important issue. The image of Lilith may arrive as you resurrect your sovereignty in the face of rejection. The image of Shiva may show you moments of awakening your inner masculine protector. Archetypal images and deities are at home expressing themselves through our moods, personalities, and complexes. Get to know your personal pantheon: Who comes through you? Who walks with you? Whom do you speak with? Honor?

DREAM TITLE   DATE

Just now I was . . .

_____

_____

_____

_____

Impressions from waking consciousness:

_____

_____

_____

Archetypes:

_____

_____

_____

Symbols:

_____

_____

_____

_____

_____

DREAM TITLE   DATE

Just now I was . . .

_____

_____

_____

_____

Impressions from waking consciousness:

_____

_____

_____

Archetypes:

_____

_____

_____

Symbols:

_____

_____

_____

_____

_____

DREAM TITLE   DATE

Just now I was . . .

_____

_____

_____

_____

Impressions from waking consciousness:

_____

_____

_____

Archetypes:

_____

_____

_____

Symbols:

_____

_____

_____

_____

_____

symbols

Part of dreamwork is working with symbols. The word symbol originates from the Late Latin symbolum, translating to creed, token, mark; or from Greek symbolon (token, watchword). Also, the prefix syn (together) combined with the suffix bole (a throwing, a casting, the stroke of a missile, bolt, beam). These etymological underpinnings provide more context and dimensionality to the word's meaning. With these roots in mind, we might understand a symbol as a token that brings together a casting, bolt, or beam. This suggests that a symbol is an invocation and a unification or transmission of energy through a physical object or visual image: the translation of a formless idea into something physical that can be universally seen or understood. Envision a lightning bolt—a giant spark of electricity bringing immense power to the collective from the great sky—to our perception, making contact with physical reality.

Historically, mythic stories and symbolic images were woven into everyday life. Humans have been evoking myths, symbols, and archetypes through art, ritual, and spiritual practice for thousands of years. Many cultures sustain themselves through common belief systems represented through a collection of symbols that can be passed down from generation to generation. Humans are essentially the same as they were thirty thousand years ago: we go through the same stages of childhood, sexual maturation, transformation into early adulthood, love, partnership, the gradual demise of the body and mind, and finally death. Because humans embody much of the same somatic responses and experiences, it makes sense that they would respond to the same images. Symbols are specific visual manifestations that can be deeply personal and yet simultaneously universal.

As Robert Moss shares, "You don't want to take the juice out of a dream symbol, by reducing it to an abstract concept." We want to amplify and honor the juicy aliveness present in this mysterious autonomous psychic force, not collapse or assassinate it. Dreams are not to be smothered and held to the unfortunate literal standards and fixed meanings that the Western world has taught us to impose upon our waking existence. Dreams are like looking at a holographic painting projected through a kaleidoscope. They are alive, moving, and changing energies within our psyches that swirl around the labyrinth of our lives. To get to know a dream one must be open, fluid, adaptable, and flexible. Grasping will only crush its wings in your closing fists. By literally representing these symbols in a physical way, through drawing or even just by looking at similar interpretations of their image, we are bringing them to life. In order to examine a dream, we must examine the context of waking consciousness and every detail of every element in the dream picture. Symbols that arise in art-making can transmit knowledge from the unconscious as a result of the ignorance of the ego and can be understood as objective representations of deep, latent, invisible conceptions with inherent and potent meaning. Jung said wisdom is to return to our personal psychic symbols and live in harmony with them.

Jung defined a symbol as the best possible representation of something that can never be fully known. This speaks to the expressiveness of symbols as well as their capacity for depth. Jung's therapeutic mode of working with dreams was to carefully go back through the dream experience and slowly begin to decrypt possible symbolic meanings. He deduced that everything within a dream was symbolic, but found that the same symbol could have many layers of meaning from the personal to the universal, making it difficult to decipher. Jung defined a symbol as "a term, a name, or an image which in itself may be familiar to us, but its connotations, use, and application are specific or peculiar and hint at a hidden, vague, or unknown meaning." He acknowledged that dreams select specific symbols to communicate the dreamer's unconscious to the dreamer alone. In his book The Dreaming Brain, American psychiatrist and dream researcher J. Allan Hobson identified the language of the dreaming mind as unique: it is represented through associations, symbols, archetypes, metaphors, and visualizations.

Characterizing them as bizarre, nonsensical, and incongruent, he noted that dreams do not show the same continuity and progression of typical waking conscious experience.

Hobson did, however, find that dreams are not entirely separate from waking consciousness. It is possible to observe the details in dreams that are from waking impressions, experiences, thoughts, and moods. Jungian theory, as psychologist Dr. Robert Van de Castle described, holds that dreams could "help sensitize us to the neglected aspects of our personality by zeroing in on blind spots in our awareness." Jung specifically said, "A dream is quite capable . . . of naming the most painful and disagreeable things without the least regard for the feelings of the dreamer." Notably, this observation concerns repressed aspects of the personality and calls attention to the ego's inability to suppress the psyche's symbolizing of unwanted unconscious material through dreams.

In this excerpt from Jung's *Memories, Dreams, Reflections*, he discussed his internal process and thoughts pertaining to uncovering the symbolic nature of dreams:

> I took great care to try to understand every single image, every
> item of my psychic inventory, and to classify them scientifically—
> so far as this was possible—and, above all, to realize them in
> actual life. . . . That is what we usually neglect to do. We allow the
> images to rise up, and maybe we wonder about them, but that is
> all. We do not take the trouble to understand them.

In his discussion in his autobiography of his confrontation with the unconscious, Jung reported that the nature of his own dreams led him to suspect that he had "some psychic disturbance," but a review of his life history revealed no evidence of this. He stated,

Thereupon I said to myself, "Since I know nothing at all, I shall simply do whatever occurs to me." Thus I consciously submitted myself to the impulses of the unconscious. As a result of my experiment I learned how helpful it can be, from the therapeutic point of view.

He claimed, "The images of the unconscious place a great responsibility upon a man. Failure to understand them . . . deprives him of his wholeness and imposes a painful fragmentariness on his life." In these statements, Jung revealed his process of doing "whatever occur[red]" and submitting to the "impulses of the unconscious," which enables the dream images to reveal themselves naturally. He stressed the notion of bringing dreams into actual life, noting that this facet of dreamwork is often neglected and that this can cause a splintering of the psyche.

Symbols are single images that represent something deeper than their literal depiction. They are expressed differently through cultures and personalities, whereas a sign is a specific symbol that operates as a substitution for direct communication. An example of a symbol is the image of a snake, which has a unique meaning dependent on the dreamer and the culture from which it arises. A sign is often portrayed as a two-dimensional graphic image, such as the biohazard design, which has a precise meaning, that being "warning, toxic or poisonous material." The difference between a symbol and a sign can be simplified this way: A symbol holds a multiplicity of meanings—it communicates something that we cannot fully conceptualize. A sign is a "stand-in" that conveys a specific meaning, like a stop sign. As Jung shared, "What we call a symbol is a term, a name, or an image which in itself may be familiar to us, but its connotations, use, and application are specific or peculiar and hint at a hidden, vague, or unknown meaning." A symbol is largely unknown.

A term or image is symbolic when it means more than it denotes or expresses. It has a wider unconscious aspect—an aspect that can never be precisely defined or fully explained. This peculiarity is due to the fact that, in exploring the symbol, the mind is finally led toward ideas of a transcendent nature, where our reason must capitulate. Because there are innumerable things beyond the range of human understanding, we constantly use symbolic expressions and images when referring to them. For example, ecclesiastical language in particular is full of symbols (think of the religious cross). The conscious use of symbolism is only one aspect of great psychological importance: we also produce symbols unconsciously and spontaneously in our dreams.

The reason our dreams speak in symbols is not because they are trying to be cryptic or elusive—it is because a symbol is actually the best way to express something that we are not yet aware of. A symbol is not a representation for the essence of something else; it is the actual thing expressing itself in the most effective language that it has. But not literally—figuratively. Symbols operate as witty, humorous, illustrious, and attention-grabbing cloaking garments for deep psychic material. Even though a symbol can seem very specific, it is also multilayered in the way that an archetype is multilayered. If you are examining a dream and you have a particular symbol that comes to you or an image that comes to you, that could be a symbol that holds your psychic energy for you. For example, imagine that you dreamed of a lion. The lion could evoke different feelings, or even a constellation of thoughts that have nothing to do with the lion itself. Maybe your mother is a Leo and that is what comes up for you—that is personal. So, while others may feel an array of other associations when they see a lion, that symbol brings with it the archetypal energy of the mother when it appears to you.

Perhaps for you, in your personal unconscious mind, the lion evokes a more archetypal matriarchal energy. There are many different layers and ways of working with symbols and archetypes within your own dreams, and through recording your dreams, you can become well versed in your own dream language. If you begin to get to know yourself and your own psychic language, then you begin to realize, oh, this is not a dream about a lion. This is a dream about my mother, and that is going to be very specific to me and my individual psyche. Everyone can have lion dreams, but what a lion means to you is going to be personal. It is so important to record your dreams and look for these markers or recurring images or symbols or archetypes. When you begin to see them, then you can begin to connect them. Jung noted that the unconscious communicates to each individual dreamer by selecting specific and unique symbols that have meaning to the dreamer and the dreamer alone. Only you know what your dream means: the irony is that often you are too close to see it clearly.

To access the completely unique and organic psychic material of the unconscious, it is helpful to meditate on one particular dream image, color, or sensation. Holding this thought in the mind with a light touch serves to distract the conscious mind from judgment and any threat of stifling the intuitive creative process. Putting aside critical thinking, the unconscious is able to speak more clearly and powerfully. One of Jung's contemporaries, John Freeman, wrote, "The dream is not a kind of standardized cryptogram that can be decoded by a glossary of symbol meanings. It is an integral, important, and personal expression of the individual unconscious." This means that generalizing the meaning of a dream is impossible because it is unique for every person. Their individual unconscious selects specific images with distinctive meaning to that individual and must be considered with particular attention. He goes on, "The dreamer's individual unconscious is communicating with the dreamer alone and is selecting symbols for its purpose that have meaning to the dreamer and to nobody else." It is therefore crucial that any person working with another's dream be highly aware of their own internalized bias, imposed meanings, and possible projections. The goal of the therapist is to guide the dreamer into their personal intrapsychic dream realm and provide new possible perspectives so that the dreamer can discover meaning for themselves.

Dream dictionaries further perpetuate wake-centric notions of consciousness. The unique expression of dream symbols and imagery cannot be subsumed by or subservient to our waking perceptions—they are a mysterious and numinous artform that transcends the ego. I chose to include the following symbol amplification, musing, suggestions, and perspectives in order to outline possibilities when encountering our dreams. These are explored from my personal experience and not intended as stagnant labels for your personal meanings. Dream symbols are not static, stationary stand-ins for meaning: they are alive, nuanced, and multilayered. Symbols are available to expand our relationship to our dreams, not to flatten or assassinate the multiplicity of our inner world. These descriptive writings are meant to expand your concept of how the multidimensional symbols in a dream might operate and what they may represent. Only you, the dreamer, know the true meaning of the dream, and the dream knows itself.

It can feel challenging to avoid getting caught up in literal interpretation and cognitive bias. Our reticular activating system, as well as our ego, loves to run the show and often has no respect for the depth of the dream or its symbols because they are under the purview of the irrational. I invite you to let go of needing to know and begin instead to explore . . .

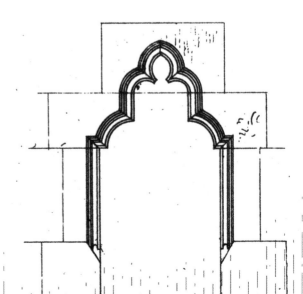

DREAM TITLE   DATE
_____

Just now I was . . .
_____
_____
_____
_____

Impressions from waking consciousness:
_____
_____
_____

Archetypes:
_____
_____
_____

Symbols:
_____
_____
_____
_____

DREAM TITLE   DATE

Just now I was . . .

Impressions from waking consciousness:

Archetypes:

Symbols:

DREAM TITLE _____   DATE _____

Just now I was . . .

_____

_____

_____

_____

Impressions from waking consciousness:

_____

_____

_____

Archetypes:

_____

_____

_____

Symbols:

_____

_____

_____

_____

DREAM TITLE   DATE

Just now I was . . .

Impressions from waking consciousness:

Archetypes:

Symbols:

DREAM TITLE   DATE

Just now I was . . .

_____

_____

_____

_____

Impressions from waking consciousness:

_____

_____

_____

_____

Archetypes:

_____

_____

_____

_____

Symbols:

_____

_____

_____

_____

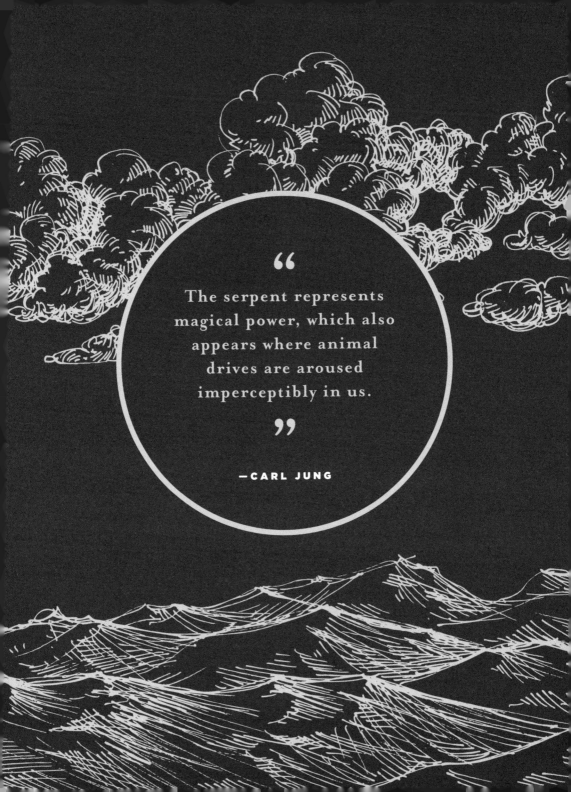

> The serpent represents magical power, which also appears where animal drives are aroused imperceptibly in us.

—CARL JUNG

SNAKE: The serpent is one of the most prominent cross-cultural symbols and has represented a medical emblem for more than twenty-four hundred years, dating back even prior to the fourth century BCE, all the way back to ancient Egypt. The reptile itself has the literal physical ability to shed its own skin. This makes it uniquely suited to represent self-regeneration over death. It is often employed to signify polar opposites such as illness and therapy, and death and rejuvenation. Snakes can represent an array of changes from transformation to descent into evil and can often embody the nonrational, creative, and supernatural qualities associated with the archetypal feminine. Themes of instinctual energy, psychological growth, regression, and creativity are all correlated with internal dream depictions of unconscious processes. Snakes can hold our deepest fears: primal nature and cold blood. Jungian Analyst Esther Harding writes, "Snakes live in dark holes and go down through cracks in the earth and in rocks. Their movement is secret and mysterious, they are cold-blooded and inaccessible to human feeling. They live in a subterranean region which to the ancients was the underworld." Slithering barely above the earth's surface, they often arrive when the psyche is ready to plumb the depths of the unconscious. After a dream snake's first appearance, dreams might begin to flood our awareness. Marie-Louise von Franz explained, "Through its ability to shed its skin, it is even immortal. But in other cultures, too, the snake plays the role of the primal enemy of the upper world of the gods: the Midgard snake, together with the Fenris wolf, threatens the gods in Asgard by creating a flood. In Greece it is Gaia, the earth goddess, who creates half-snakes, the Titans, who storm Olympus and wrestle with Zeus. Simultaneously, she is the mother of Echidna (snake), of the Sphinx, Cerberus, and others. Leviathan, too, the antagonist of Jehovah, is a snake, a dragon at the bottom of the sea." She goes on, "It is quite clear from this compilation of images that the snake symbolizes the vital, instinctual, and drive stirrings in man, his unconscious dark side in contrast to brightness, to the conscious side of his nature." Snakes are potent dream visitors sharing eons of collective mythology. Jung called them the single most common symbol of transcendence. What type of snake arrived in your dream? Was it a cobra? A kingsnake? A ball python?

OCEAN: Its mysterious depths flood us with tidal waves of dreams, instincts, and emotions. The power of the ocean is unparalleled. Dip your toes into the unknown. The salty ionized air relieves tension and circular thinking, inviting you to surrender and let go. The ocean embodies our unconscious, all that is beyond our conscious grasp and comprehension. We cannot dominate or understand the sheer magnitude of this magical force. It rejects our every attempt to control nature. Its power calls to us through the reverberation of the heartbeat that we hear inside of seashells, and the crests of its waves remind us that we are just small incarnations of a vast elemental all. In the depths of the sea, there are literally living fossils, complete ecosystems unscathed by the sun's rays.

This complex world remains largely unchanged, similar to the archaic and archetypal lattice that remains underneath the organizing systems of our psyches—our mind is like the very bottom of the deep blue sea. The salt water is akin to amniotic fluid, our place of initial inception, and to our body's naturally cleansing tears. We are made of water, pulled like the ocean by the tidal waves tethered to the celestial cycles of the moon. The ocean is the great mother, the ancient primordial feminine, fluid and crushing. She permits and punishes. We are just tiny droplets carried by her magnitude and majesty. For the mystics, the image of the ocean connects to infinity and a union with the divine. There might be a change coming, lapping at your ankles and calling you inward . . . when we dream of oceans, we are being told that we must rise from the depths and become a new being. In a dream, oceans can parallel the depths of the unconscious and emotionality, the shifting of tides and the changing of moods. Notice details: the color of the water, the temperature, the mood, and the depth. Is it a raging sea? A calm balmy shallow tide pool?

Turquoise waters descending into a kelp forest? The ocean speaks to us through dreams. Listen.

DROWNING: Drowning is terrifying. Think of tidal waves and stormy seas. Drowning is a type of suffocation induced by the submersion or immersion of the mouth and nose in a liquid. The lack of oxygen is fatal. Historically and mythologically, mass drownings have been used to destroy and punish humanity. Drowning metaphorically might convey ultimate despair, loss, and suicidal thoughts. In modern language, "drowning" can mean being completely overwhelmed. We drown in emotions, paperwork, adulting, workload, and more. In dreams, drowning can convey a softening of the personality, a dissolution causing the psyche to weaken and lose its foundation. This can appear as a psychological emergence or at the precipice of a psychotic break. As Edward Edinger shared concerning drowning in dreams as connected to the alchemical process of Solutio, "Solutio is a major alchemical image and it is likewise extremely important psychologically. The basic images that refer to this symbol system are such things as swimming in water, bathing, showering, maybe drowning, dissolution; but also baptism and rejuvenation through the process, through the ordeal by water. Solutio is an image of a descent into the unconscious that has the effect of dissolving the solid, ordered structure of the ego." It can symbolize an ego death, dispersal, or dissolution. Drowning is losing one's footing, regaining consciousness through a rebirth or psychic baptism. Drowning suggests a plunge into unconsciousness that is not mitigated by breaths on the surface of consciousness. Something is plummeting you deep into the depths without air—how might you be feeling submerged or suffocated? How can you be gentle with yourself and breathe? An aspect wants to emerge, coagulate, or be reborn.

"The psychotic drowns in the same waters in which the mystic swims with delight."

—Joseph Campbell

BLACK PANTHER: The first time I dreamed about a black jaguar was in my early twenties. She was chasing me through a wild jungle, and I ran into an abandoned cabin and hid under a bunk bed to escape her. She followed me and sat patiently next to the bed. I thought she was going to kill me. Her voice whispered inside my head and summoned me to come out of hiding. I slid outward across the floor and prepared to embrace my death. She slowly climbed on top of me and enveloped me with her black velvet body. We merged into each other, I was her and she was me. . . . The panther or black jaguar often represents reclaiming one's true power. Jaguars are connected to the hidden secrets of earth and they often arrive as an adept guide through twilight and the chthonic, or underworld, realms. She is associated with the darkness of the new moon and winter. A symbol of her ferocity and valor, she is the aggressive aspect and power of lunar consciousness. The panther is usually smaller but fiercer than lions and even tigers. She's an incredible multitasker physically, mentally, psychically, and spiritually. Panthers are loners— they are solitary and enchanting. In dreams, panthers often arrive to lead us toward the development of greater depth and enhance our inner knowing. They come to guide us into the psychic underworld and help magnify multidimensional communications. Panthers are fearless, aggressive, and sensitive; they listen intently to their environment and poise themselves with divine timing. Associated with winter and the new moon, panthers gather power in the hours of darkness. They have the ability to bite through the skull of their prey and emulate what it truly means to embody one's power through skill, grace, precision, and intuition. Often the arrival of a black panther can symbolize a deep stirring in the unconscious psyche, an awakening to new levels of magic and mysticism.

PEARL: Natural pearls are treasures from the depths. Historically, they have adorned royalty and ornamented kings, queens, and even the pope. Undersea pearls are protected by mermaids and water nymphs. Pearl necklaces caress deities in strands, strung around their bodies like tiny orbs of divine light. Pearls are alchemical in nature—what might begin as a tiny bit of sand or dirt enters the shell, and then concentric layers of calcium carbonate called "nacre" slowly build around it like the rings of a tree. Eventually, completely enveloped, this tiny piece of grit becomes a beautiful iridescent wonder of nature, a pearl. They are the "pearls of wisdom" that emerge from the depths of the oceanic unconscious. They can be connected with the archetype of the Self and sacred feminine. In China and India, pearls are regarded as a symbol of immortality, and in Greece they are a symbol of love. In the modern Jewish mystical practice of Kedumah, the quality of divine presence experienced through embodied human consciousness as an expression of being is called "Pearl," which comes from the ancient Hebrew tradition. My mysticism teacher Zvi Ish-Shalom wrote, "The pearl grows like an embryo in the wound of our soul." Pearls might suggest a baby gestating in their mother's womb, the origin of spirits' inception in matter. They are a sparkled speck of light cradled in the darkness of the ocean's bottom. The ocean floor is unknown; this subterranean landscape holds our deepest fears, instincts, passions, potential, and precious treasures. Pearls imbue a soft, pastel-hued, youthful glow, often a gift of purity or expressed through a bride's necklace. This almost virginal quality is contrasted by its constitution: the oyster, a hardened shell with a fleshy inside, hidden in the deepest psychic depths of the sea of mystery.

TWINS: Life itself comes from the double helix of our DNA. We are born of pairs and opposites—the whole of the living human world is dependent on the symbol of the double. Twins appear frequently in folk cosmologies, often cast in morally opposing roles. Twins in mythology have been illustrated as two halves of the same whole, sharing a bond deeper than that of ordinary siblings, or as fierce rivals. They can represent twin aspects of the self, doppelgängers, or the shadow. Twins in waking life can also be shown to have special or paranormal powers and deep bonds. Carl Jung discussed the power and meaning of opposites at length. These pairs of syzygies arise out of humanity's primordial awareness that day is paired with night, light with darkness, and summer with winter. The archetype of twins simultaneously expresses both opposites and sameness. Two bodies, one womb, together representing a whole and individuals. For Jung the opposites were "the ineradicable and indispensable preconditions of all psychic life. In their natural state, they coexist in an undifferentiated way. The tension between these two continues to percolate, culminate, and gestate until a new psychic force is born. This process, according to Jung, is the transcendent function. This function serves to transform energy that is dormant in the unconscious mind due to

the splitting off into the unconscious of content that is too distressing to consciously integrate. Thinking about the twos and the tarot, we see the gathering of information before full realization. We have passivity and reception, a pause before action, and the presence of duality. Matter is inert but in preparation for something new, the germination of the third.

BUTTERFLY: Butterflies are a feminine symbol in Japanese culture associated with happiness. They are connected to resurrection and immortality, as they seemingly die and are born again. Often butterflies express an experience of liberation, new beginnings, and transformation. "Butterfly" can be translated into the Greek word *psyche.* It is said that the myth of Psyche and Eros expresses the union of the heart and soul. In the myth, adapted by Paul Carus, before descending into the tomb, Psyche says, "Remember that my name is a prophecy. It links my destiny with invisible but strong ties to the fate of the dainty butterfly. A groveling grub entombs herself as a chrysalis in the cocoon, whence she comes forth a being of celestial beauty, whose body seems to consist of pure ether and rainbow colors, a winged flower, a living parable of profound sentiment and a fitting emblem of the human soul." From ancient to modern times the butterfly has shown us not only the power of physical metamorphosis, but as psyche, also the beautiful metaphorical transmigration of the human soul. On February 11, 2018, I dreamed that I was in a Kabbalah class where my sparkly skinned, bejeweled professor was discussing the transmigration of human souls through the form of butterflies. In honoring each individual's psyche, soul, and butterfly it is possible to see the truly transformative nature of the human spirit. We are not static, we are ever evolving. Jungian Analyst Murray Stein integrates the symbol of the butterfly throughout the book *Transformation: Emergence of the Self*, writing, "When the caterpillar hears the call, it begins preparing for pupation. The change that now transforms the caterpillar into a pupa is of far greater magnitude than any other molts it has undergone previously. . . . Complete metamorphosis is a dramatic transformation, out of which a creature emerges that bears no resemblance to the one that existed before. Who would guess, just by looking at it, that a swiftly darting moth or butterfly once was a thick worm lumbering heavily along the ground?" The blue morpho butterfly, for example, is among the largest species in the world, with wings spanning anywhere from five to eight inches. The morpho's vivid, iridescent blue coloring is a result of the microscopic scales on their wings, which reflect light the color of the sky. These butterflies can symbolize change or rebirth, the flight of the soul, and a shift in consciousness. Blue butterflies are often considered a symbol of love and can send us a vibration of joy and happiness.

LABYRINTH: Labyrinths range from two-dimensional symmetrical patterns to three-dimensional intricate mazes to multi-dimensional symbols for the psychospiritual human experience.

The labyrinth is an ancient symbol and mirrors the archetype of spiraling shapes that arrive through nature's beauty in sea shells, whirlpools, fern tendrils, and spiral galaxies. Labyrinths have been found carved into archaic figurines, painted on cave walls, and etched into stone and marble churches, courtyards, and on gothic cathedral floors. Labyrinth precursors were visible on Mycenaean seals and early Egyptian amulet fragments. In medieval times, labyrinth floors served to host religious dances. One of the most prominent mythological symbols, they often emerge through dreams, perhaps as a winding spiral staircase, a library corridor, or an amusement park waterslide. James Hillman noted, "the soul draws us through the labyrinth . . . ever inward" as dreams themselves also do. Jung stated that "one of the fundamental laws of natural development is that it moves in a spiral, and the true law of nature is always reached after the labyrinth has been traveled."

Labyrinths draw us ever toward their alluring center as we meander the circuitous paths of our lives and personal individuation processes. Jungian psychologist Joseph Lewis Henderson and anthropologist Maud Oakes discussed the psychological symbology of the labyrinth, writing, "in the traversal of the labyrinth, there is brought about that particular loss of ego-consciousness necessary for any fundamental change to take place. . . . The symbolism of a return to the prenatal condition, so abundantly suggested in the composite idea of the labyrinth (intestines, birth canal, umbilical cord, etc.) and water (water of death or water of life as amniotic fluid), vanishes from sight and the evidence of rebirth becomes apparent." A labyrinth might suggest a birth portal or new adventure. While the contractions within this cosmic canal might feel harrowing, this image directly connects us to our experience of Self and of life. As artist and writer Jess Horkey so eloquently shared, "We are all in the labyrinth together, all in the spiral, all in the gyre, and it's terrifying and also beautiful too, because that's what being alive is. Both."

CROCODILE: Crocodiles are essentially living dinosaurs, having been around for about 230 million years. When encountering reptiles in dreams, I am often reminded of the "reptilian brain": the brainstem, basal ganglia, and cerebellum, which are largely responsible for our primal behaviors and trauma responses, often summarized as "feed, fight, flight, and fornication." When these powerful reptilian forces arrive in a dream, they might be holding an energy that is ancient. Astronomer Carl Sagan wrote, "Deep inside the skull of every one of us there is something like a brain of a crocodile. Surrounding the R-complex [Reptilian complex] is the limbic system or mammalian brain, which evolved tens of millions of years ago in ancestors who were mammal but not yet primates. It is a major source of our moods and emotions, of our concern and care for the young." The ancient Egyptian goddess Ammit has the head of a crocodile and will swallow your heart if you fail to achieve psychic balance within your lifetime and your heart is too heavy on the scales of justice. Crocodiles are extremely armored to protect their sensitive underbelly. They have incredible night vision, allowing them to peer into the depths of the darkness. Crocodiles are versatile creatures, thriving in both fresh and salt water. They are also able to traverse the land. They are present across cultures and are associated with power, agility, and the wisdom of the primordial earth and underworld. The Egyptian deity Geb embodies the form of a crocodile stationed at the threshold of the underworld. The god Sobek, too, is depicted as a crocodile and lords over the organization of the entire universe. Sobek was also a fertility god, connecting crocodile again to the lush, generative, and fecund ground of the earth. If you have dreamed of a crocodile, be curious about the divine, ancient, primordial part of yourself that is well protected but possibly wants to initiate you into accessing repressed unconscious material.

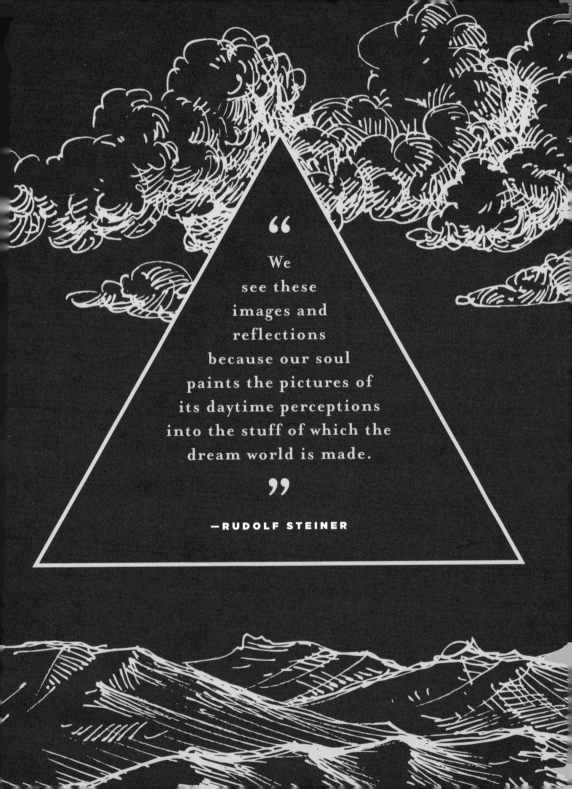

"

We
see these
images and
reflections
because our soul
paints the pictures of
its daytime perceptions
into the stuff of which the
dream world is made.

"

—RUDOLF STEINER

DREAM ALTAR

Making a dream altar is a beautiful offering to your dreams. It can be simple or extravagant. This is a space to honor, incubate, and tend to your dream space. This is an intentional space where you can direct meaningful objects or tools or even simply a single image that inspires you in a way that cultivates a sacred and specific place where you are allowing your dreams to feel honored and to consciously invite them to show up to you more fully. This is a space dedicated to your dream practice.

A dream altar might be placed near your bed or in a separate room that is intentionally curated for spiritual work or introspection. Set your space with an altar cloth; it could be cotton or silk or any fabric that you associate with dreams, maybe something soft or even fluffy. It might be white, blue, silver, black, or even purple or printed with stars. Think about colors that connect with dreaming and your intention for your personal dream practice. On this altar you may place tools specific to your ancestral tradition or practice working with dreams; photographs of powerful dreamers, dreamworkers, deities, or elders; dream herbs; candles; tinctures; spagyrics (alchemical preparations of tinctures and ointments); ointments; oils; stones; or anything else that feels intuitive or unique to your own relationship with dreaming.

To show the dream that you are listening, you might intentionally wear an item of clothing that was from your dream or call a friend that was in your dream. Or you could honor the dream more deeply by recording your dream, meditating, leaving offerings, asking questions, or simply spending the time to examine and explore the dream in your mind. You might work the dream or draw the dream. You could even look up dream images online, as long as you're not digesting them too literally and clinging to a direct and inflexible interpretation. For example, if you had a dream about a castle, just looking at images of castles can show your psyche that you have dedicated time to bringing those images into your waking conscious awareness.

You can write or list your waking emotions and experience as you work with the dream, as well as the associations that you have drawn from it. You might consider what actions you can participate in during your waking life that relate to your dream content. This is one of my favorite things to do. For example, if I have a dream that I am eating a chocolate bar, the next day, I will most certainly go get a chocolate bar and eat it. This is a very useful and practical way to show the dream that you are paying attention. Listen, honor what you have seen and heard, and let the dream come forward. Don't take the dream *too* literally, of course—you don't need to buy a race car if you dream of one—but there are plenty of ways to honor the dream symbols that you have encountered while asleep at night into your waking life.

dreams are like art

One of the biggest traps that I encounter with folks during the process of doing dreamwork is that they assume and often literalize everything. For example, if they dream about their friend, they think, "Oh, this is a dream about my friend. So, it's a dream about my friend." In reality, when you have dreams in which certain people appear, those people's presence could be one of the layers of the dream, but the dream is probably not about those people specifically. That is actually not how a dream generally works. Dreams are like paintings. When you see a painting of a bowl of fruit, what you are seeing is not actually a bowl or fruit. To say that the painting was in fact a bowl of fruit would be to be mistaking it, right?

A painting is a whole artistic expression. It is paint. It is pigment. It is canvas, paper, cloth, or wood. It is mood lighting, a time and a space, illustrating something much deeper that comes from a feeling. One way that I describe this in metaphorical simplistic terms is that art is both an object itself and a symbolic representation or expression of many other aspects of an experience. A painting of a house, for example, is not a literal house. Rather, it evokes a mood, a time, a place, feelings, politics, a narrative . . . to mistake the painting for a house is to completely miss its deep and symbolic layers of meaning. When you look at a painting and ask the artist, "What does it mean?" you are asking them to translate something into words that is not fully expressible in words.

Dreams serve as an artistic bridge directly to the unconscious. They are powerful expressions of our inner and spiritual worlds. In working with dreams we peel back their many layers, so when someone shares, "Oh, I had a dream about my friend," take multiple factors into consideration. Ask yourself whether this might be a prophetic dream, or literal, or strictly metaphorical. If it is not a prophetic dream or literal, then we need to approach the dream symbolically, which is often the case. I encourage the dreamer to let their immediate desire for an explanation go so that we can examine their dream in a way that we might a piece of art. For example, what feeling did the dream have? What emotion did that conjure? How were the people in the dream presented? What did they look like? Were they younger or older? Were they wearing certain things? What was the mood of the space? Those kinds of questions help us get away from the literalization of the characters in a dream and often show us our complexes.

Many people want to know what their dream symbols mean, and look to the internet or dream dictionaries. Generally, what this does is completely reduce a multidimensional piece of art to a simple conceptual statement. It's like saying, "This painting is about the juxtaposition of sadness and anger." That is a statement—a statement that your conceptual mind understands—but when you look at a painting, perhaps you feel something that you can't quite explain. That is what is important. You are seeking that feeling and the totality of the experience, which touches not only your mind but also your body and soul.

Dream symbols are the artistic expression of your spirit. They are a culmination of your personal emotions, experiences, and collective amplifications. Here is a poignant example. If someone tells me they dreamed of water, I'll want to know details. What kind of water? Where were you? Was it hot or cold? Day or night? They describe a vast sea. Google says the sea represents your calm mind and influx of emotions. But we go deeper. Is it a sea or is it the ocean? Big difference there. It's a sea. Okay, I ask: Is it the Red Sea? Or possibly the Mediterranean? These are important details, because each symbol carries a lifetime of mythos, ancestral history, and personal associations. Maybe you are Jewish, maybe you work with Lilith, maybe when you were young you physically went to the Red Sea and immediately, subsequently experienced trauma. . . . These details affect the interpretation. The more we explore, the more we can understand why your dream painted this particular film behind your eyes while you slept.

DREAM TIPS

STAYING AWAY FROM JUDGMENT

To access the completely unique and organic psychic material of the unconscious, it is helpful to meditate on one particular dream image, color, or sensation. Holding this thought in the mind with a light touch aids to distract the conscious mind from judgment and from stifling the intuitive creative process. Putting aside critical thinking and judgment, the unconscious is able to speak more clearly and more powerfully.

STAYING IN THE ROOM

If a particular thought, feeling, emotion, interaction, or experience begins to invite anxiety or panic, try to focus on the beauty and details of the space around you, the chairs, the lights, your feet feeling the floor underneath you, to sense smells, or to feel textures. Ground yourself in your body in the here and now. Notice physical sensations and visual information. Try to connect with your own breath. Breathe and affirm to yourself that you are in a safe space.

STAYING AWAY FROM EGO TRIPS

In his book *Inner Work*, Robert Johnson discusses a few things to avoid when extracting meaning from your dreams. One would be choosing an interpretation that boosts your own ego; often dreams are showing us things that we do not already know and highlighting more shadowy or unconscious areas for us to investigate and address to continue our self-development. Johnson also mentions that you should avoid interpretations that release you of self-responsibility. Dreams are not there to prove us right; they do not act as a value system that judges others; they only show us our own projections.

DREAM TITLE   DATE

Just now I was . . .

_____

_____

_____

_____

Impressions from waking consciousness:

_____

_____

_____

_____

Archetypes:

_____

_____

_____

_____

Symbols:

_____

_____

_____

_____

_____

DREAM TITLE   DATE

Just now I was . . .

_____

_____

_____

_____

Impressions from waking consciousness:

_____

_____

_____

Archetypes:

_____

_____

_____

Symbols:

_____

_____

_____

_____

DREAM TITLE   DATE

Just now I was . . .

_____

_____

_____

_____

Impressions from waking consciousness:

_____

_____

_____

Archetypes:

_____

_____

_____

Symbols:

_____

_____

_____

_____

dreaming, artistic practice, and creative flow

This journal is a dream art journal. Deepening your understanding of the physiological and psychological relationship between dreams and arts practice can illuminate and inform your experience of transforming your dreams through various media. I want to take space to outline some of the research that highlights our dreaming mind's natural propensity toward healing, connection to the body, and creativity in an attempt to scaffold your psyche as you begin to bring your dreams onto the page.

Dreams are not bound by time and space. Our consciousness turns back on itself, and our unconscious mind's inner artist is set free. Creativity is similar to dreams, as they are both living energies with their own movement and intelligence. C. F. Kwiatkowski and J. F. Pagel studied creativity and dreaming and reported, "The dream is the illumination component of the creative process and it serves as a spiritually or intellectually enlightening experience that can both inspire and inform creative work." Psychologist Kelly Bulkeley suggested that the connection between art and dreaming is deep and possibly goes as far back as the Upper Paleolithic period sixty thousand years ago. He noted that cave paintings during this period contain many of the prominent themes found in dreams. The purposes of this creative intersection have not been explicitly explored or expressed within dominant and contemporary culture. Although artists throughout time have conjured images from their dreams and used them to inspire their creative work, dreaming has more recently been discovered as an integral aspect of the creative process.

The inherent symbolism, archetypal imagery, and visual presentation of dreams closely connects dream psychology to the artistic process. The clear association between dreaming and creativity suggests that dreaming has an active and functional role in creative practice. This is such an exciting space of exploration for creative dreamers. Social psychologist Graham Wallas described the four parts of the creative process as preparation, incubation, illumination, and verification. I find this to be a helpful, digestible framework. Sleep researchers James Pagel and C. F. Kwiatkowski deeply studied creativity and dreaming, sharing, "The dream is the illumination component of the creative process and it serves as a spiritually or intellectually enlightening experience that can both inspire and inform creative work." They described dreaming as a cognitive process that has many functions promoting the proliferation of creativity: It can assimilate environmental experiences in a medium free of logical constraints, it serves to expand and cultivate new information, it integrates external reality into memory, and it can function "as a metaphorical attempt at problem solving." In their research concerning the integration of dreams into artwork and creative practices, they found that "individuals with product-oriented creative interests are more likely to have . . . 'impactful' dreams and use their dreams in their lives."

The artistic and creative process can also be correlated with a state of flow. Flow theory was initiated by psychologist Mihaly Csikszentmihalyi in 1975 and held that creative activity can actually influence emotional affect by eliciting the experience of flow. Flow is defined as "an automatic, effortless, yet highly focused state of consciousness" and has been conceptualized as a particular type of optimal experience associated with vital engagement, which is a deep involvement in activities that are significant to the self and that promote feelings of aliveness and vitality. Becoming rapt in the creative process triggers a flow state of deep focus and concentration, and flow during visual creativity is directly correlated with an increased positive mood and stress reduction. You may recall a feeling of being in flow during a creative project, riding a bicycle, cooking, or engaging in any activity that simultaneously challenges you and brings you alive.

One of the ways a state of flow can facilitate stress reduction is by inducing transient hypofrontality, a term put forth by Arne Dietrich, a psychologist interested in cognitive neuroscience and philosophical psychology. He explained that in transient hypofrontality, the brain downregulates and thus conserves energy. He proposed that when the brain is under pressure, it begins to reserve its limited metabolic resources for only its most critical processes, which results in the downregulation of neural structures whose calculations are not direly needed for the present task. This theory suggests that certain areas of the brain decrease excessive neural activity. Dietrich noted, for example, that people with posttraumatic stress disorder commonly have an overactive amygdala, leading to stress and hyperarousal. He found that if the amygdala loses metabolic resources, it becomes impossible for it to sustain unnecessary neural overactivity, which can lead to an experience of lowered anxiety and de-stress. Dietrich expressed some of the emotional and cognitive implications of hypofrontality:

> [Hypofrontality] exerts some of its anxiolytic and antidepressant effects by inhibiting the excessive neural activity in ventromedial prefrontal cortex regions, and thus reducing the relative imbalance between ventromedial prefrontal cortex and dorsolateral prefrontal cortex activity. . . . [This] makes it impossible for the brain to sustain excessive neural activity in structures, such as the prefrontal cortex and the amygdala, that are not needed at that time. The brain must shunt resources away from the very structures that compute the information engendering stress, anxiety and negative thinking.

To explain succinctly, when your brain cannot sustain output, it can begin to divert activation from areas that induce stress responses. Understanding how transient hypofrontality affects brain functioning in a flow state helps explain how flow can mitigate mental distress. Steven Kotler, founder of the Flow Research Collective, and Jamie Wheal, an expert specializing in the neuroscience and application of flow states, further discussed at length the neuroanatomy of flow states and how they affect the brain's health as well as its creative abilities.

They explained that flow causes deactivation in the brain, and the brain begins to switch from conscious processing, which is extremely slow and energy-expensive, to subconscious processing, which is quick and energy-efficient. According to Kotler, large areas of the brain shut down during transient hypofrontality, including the dorsolateral prefrontal cortex, which is responsible for self-monitoring and impulse control. This causes self-consciousness to dissolve and increases creativity and openness as one is liberated from the inner self-critic. This can feel like a process of letting go or surrendering; deeply immersed in an attentionally engaging and slightly challenging activity, we stop assigning critical values to our experience, such as "good" or "bad," and feel the freedom of being inextricably linked to the present moment.

Kotler stated that the neurochemistry of a flow state includes production of five of the most potent neurochemicals—norepinephrine, dopamine, anandamide, endorphins, and serotonin—which are known to enhance performance and focus. All of these neurochemicals are potent reward chemicals that impact our motivation. Kotler discussed how creativity escalates in these states exponentially due to norepinephrine and dopamine tightening focus, allowing the brain to take in more information per second and thus heightening the access to novel thoughts. You may have a sudden insight or idea or solution that seemingly comes out of nowhere. He explained that norepinephrine and serotonin increase focus by lowering signal-to-noise ratios in the brain, which also enhances pattern recognition. This helps us more easily connect our thoughts and their helpful relationships with one another. According to Kotler, anandamide is a known pain reliever but also increases the linking of disparate ideas present in lateral thinking. Increased pattern recognition and lateral thinking enable the brain's neural networks to cross-communicate in new, highly focused ways, which results in maximized creative ability. Kotler observed that the state of flow completely envelops the creative process; people are so significantly more creative in a state of flow that this heightened creativity outlasts the flow state itself by a few days, suggesting that being in a state of flow actually trains the brain to be more creative. Dreaming and subsequently making art could be viewed as a superpower that increases cognizance and intelligence, and strengthens the immune system.

In a qualitative study by occupational therapy specialists Frances Reynolds and Sarah Prior examining the role of flow-state experiences during visual art-making in women with cancer, flow was observed through self-reported experiences of creative license and adventure that enabled spontaneous discovery. These experiences seemed to act as an antidote to the "helplessness and psychological confinement that are common for people living with cancer." The participants expressed that they felt connected to the art-making experience through "sensuous vitality," which was generated from their physical and psychological interactions with vibrant colors and textures through the artistic process. Reynolds and Prior concluded that these experiences immersed the women deeply in the present moment of flow and redirected their attention away from any intrusive thoughts about their major illness. During hypofrontality and flow, "the brain sustains massive and widespread neural activation that runs motor units, assimilates sensory inputs and coordinates autonomic regulation." This explanation points to how the participants in Reynolds and Prior's study were able to be so deeply absorbed in the now while still having such high creative activation.

The dominant creative expression upon which art depends to initiate therapeutic effects includes complex neurological processes in many areas of the brain. In artistic practice, the entire brain and body are involved in the creation of "complex intersubjective, perceptual, intrapsychic, physical, and artistic processes," and "because it promotes creativity in multi-integrative ways, art can be considered a whole brain activity that does not depend on any single area or process in the brain," as described by Dr. Gioia Chilton, a board-certified art therapist. Considering the level of complex interconnected neural, biological, and psychological processes present, flow states could lay vital groundwork for emerging therapeutic benefits of the creative art experience. In facilitating the artistic process, the therapist has the opportunity to help individuals enter and maintain a flow state that can lead to an increased sense of well-being.

art therapy: physiology of the imagination

In my undergraduate psychology program, I minored in art therapy. Before then, I had never even heard of art therapy, and I was delightedly blown away to discover that there was such an incredible body of work legitimizing artistic practice within the therapeutic container. Art therapy is a mind-body intervention as well as a certified method of psychotherapy, and its earliest roots are steeped in the work of Carl Jung. Vija Lusebrink, an art therapist, observed that images serve as "a bridge between body and mind," directly affecting the cognitive levels of information processing and physiological somatic sensations in the body. Lusebrink highlighted using guided imagery in conjunction with the tangible creation of expressive arts and described guided imagery as an experiential process whereby an individual is led into relaxation through a set of directives and then, in a receptive state of mind, is suggested to imagine specific images. She noted that this practice has been shown to reduce symptoms of stress, elevate moods, and enhance the immune system's natural ability to heal.

As Lusebrink explained, just as in a dream, the body responds to the perceived stimuli of the imagination in almost exactly the same way as it would to the physical stimuli in present direct experience. She cited research showing that both the imagery that humans see and the imagery that they imagine activate similar aspects of the visual cortex and that the physical body responds to mental depictions as if they were actually happening in reality. She reported that researchers have found that visualizing healing images has a profound effect on the physical body, including a strengthened immune system, lowered blood pressure, and lower pulse rate. According to Lusebrink, when seeing images in reality through the imagination, as well as through memory and in dreams, the brain's neurons send signals to the body in response to the images. First the messages travel to the lower part of the brain connected to the hypothalamus. The hypothalamus then signals the parasympathetic nervous system to lower blood pressure, slow breathing, and decrease heart rate. Lusebrink suggested that doing visualization with the imagination can be therapeutic and release physical tension trapped in the body.

How the brain functions and how it influences emotions, cognition, and behavior are vital components in the treatment of the most common psychological maladies brought into therapy, including mood disorders, posttraumatic stress, addictions, and physical illness. A study by arts-based research health specialist Paul Camic showed that creating visual art coupled with cognitive behavioral therapeutic techniques, guided imagery, and meditation resulted in reduced physical chronic pain in participating adults. This assertion is based on research that images, observed and imagined, have a profound therapeutic effect on the body and the psyche. Using creative imagination to create art is both an internal and external process that has the capability to renew the personality. By more intimately understanding how our mind, body, and consciousness work together, we can begin to allow our dream consciousness and creative practice to heal us in ways we have never imagined.

dream sketches

Keep in mind, when remembering a dream through doodling, drawing, or any art-making process, you are literally "putting it back together." Image-making is a powerful exercise of letting our unconscious create union out of the mysterious symbols that dwell within us and expressing them on the physical plane.

Draw or sketch your dream here:

Draw or sketch your dream here:

Draw or sketch your dream here:

The many ways that Carl Jung used creative art therapy and psychotherapy in his practice of active imagination were a large influence on modern art therapists. Jung's artwork illustrating his dreams and active imaginations in his personal work with his unconscious is documented in *The Red Book*. Similar to guided imagery, active imagination utilizes functions of our substrate levels of awareness, subconscious, and even elements of unconsciousness. Jung detailed that active imagination is "a sequence of fantasies produced by deliberate concentration on a particular image." Through active imagination, a client or individual observes movement and change in their psyche during a meditation on a particular image.

Jung suggested choosing a single image from a dream and introspectively noting subtle psychic changes. Art therapist Shaun McNiff described this process as "an inner drama involving the full spectrum of artistic expressions," suggesting that active imagination can grant access to a multitude of creative forces that may have previously been unconscious. Active imagination is a process of imaginal dialogue like guided imagery, but has less conscious direction and intervention. It is a meditative self-introspective inquiry that can be used to reimagine into the dream picture, exposing latent feelings and symbols, as well as a creative process that takes "place both before and after artistic image making occurs and involves interacting with the art object through the imagination and in response, creating another series of visual expressions."

Jungian analyst Robert Bosnak revealed a similar process that he called "embodied imagination," which served to highlight the embodied experience of autonomous dream elements. Bosnak wrote, "The most absolute and unmediated form of embodied imagination is a dream." He suggested that dreams themselves arise in images "that embody their own active intelligence" and are substantial forms of creative imagination. Bosnak suggested that "an embodied image comes to life by possessing us. Upon being absorbed in its medium, we become the medium of its epiphany." He likened this experience to that of "mixed media" and claimed that "embodiment is the fundamental archaic way of knowing.

Embodiment precedes mental and emotional knowing." Bosnak noted that "especially in dreams, it is clear how powerful the imagination is—it is capable of shaping a completely real world, indistinguishable from the physical world." This confirms that even moving your hand over a piece of paper as a physical act could evoke and transmute pieces of the dream experience.

Psychoanalyst Leanne Domash writes about and explores Bosnak's technique of embodied imagination in her article "Dreamwork and Transformation: Facilitating Therapeutic Change Using Embodied Imagination." She explains, "In the work of Embodied Imagination . . . as the patient embodies the dream image through empathic identification—enters the image and feels it in the body—the patient is employing an open and fluid use of metaphor." She further states that metaphor is the language of the emotional brain "that unconsciously categorizes emotional experience by establishing similarities and differences between past and present. Our early memories are linked to consciousness through metaphor, and the open and fluid use of metaphor is fundamental to the development of the imagination." Domash discusses how the presymbolic schemas of dreams mirror the language of preverbal developmental imprints, suggesting that early memory structures, patterns, and ideas could be accessed and reprocessed through dreamwork. This is powerful information that suggests that it is possible to process birth trauma, insidious developmental imprints from our intrauterine and postnatal experiences and environments, through our imagination and embodied dreamwork. She describes this recontextualization: "During the dreamwork, she or he enters many different types of images but remains oneself at the same time, experiencing a dual consciousness, a sense of similarity while maintaining difference." Using these techniques, it is possible to deepen psychological engagement and amplify a variety of spontaneous unconscious material and a diverse spectrum of expressions. This capacity of active and embodied imagination makes them complementary to dreamwork in therapeutic practice.

are you
ready
to dive
into your
dreams?!

find a comfortable seat.
Feel your body make contact with the physical world.

The sensation of gravity's hug, cradling your tender form.

I would invite you to take a deep, expansive breath, all the way into your low belly.

Bringing oxygen into the crevices of your sacred soma, allowing every cell in your body to breathe.

I invite you to connect softly with your heart space.

Holding the inspirited fire of life within its warm, rhythmic center.

Continuing to breathe and allowing your shoulders to slowly drop and relaxing your jaw and face.

Let your eyelids be heavy, let your thoughts dissipate, like listless clouds moving across a night sky. Imagine that you are in the most comfortable and lustrous sleeping space.

Your head, embraced by soft pillows, your body supported by soothing blankets or peaceful sensations.

Breathe deeply as you bring your attention toward the blackness of inner space.

A pool of water emerges in your mind's eye.

Let the calm, fluid, and oceanic image of the depths call you inward.

Stepping into the pool, you feel the watery unconscious tug on the soles of your feet.

You are now at the precipice of sleep, the liminal in-between space of potent dreams.

Make the choice to submerge yourself through this portal and dive into the realm of dreaming.

You begin to feel your body sinking, slowly and gently, into the dark night sky.

Swathed in delicate fabric, you float into the darkness, enveloped by spaciousness, caressed by the dancing sea of twinkling stars.

As you descend, feel your body gain density as gravity pulls you toward the beckoning surface of the earth.

As your feet touch the ground, you open your awareness to reveal the place of the dream.

Gradually lift the gaze of your inner eyes and notice where you have arrived.

Bringing the elements of the dreamscape slowly into focus, observe.

Are you outside or inside?

What time of day is it?

Looking around, from left to right, forward and behind, what do you see?

What energies, beings, characters, figures, objects, or structures might you notice?

Allow the softness of the dream to appear more and more clear.

Details emerge that you passed over before, and something or someone draws your attention.

Notice what in the dream carries the most charge, an energy or magnetic call to your awareness. It pulls you closer. Walking toward this image, allowing your mind to open and your heart to expand in curiosity, continue to bring the experience into focus.

If you approach an object, what is it? Turn it over in your hands or vision.

If you address a person or energy, who are they?

Introduce yourself, and politely inquire why they might be appearing.

Once you have allowed images to arise from your unconscious mind, the goal is to begin to listen to them deeply. Our inner figures move of their own volition, and it is not our job to tamper with them. Often, they will say things that we do not like or offer us information that we do not feel ready to receive. This is the power of dreamwork. When we dialogue with our inner images, they can show us deep aspects of our repressed selves. See if you can stay present with a single image or a feeling and let it unearth itself and communicate with you intuitively. Experience it without moving away from it, avoiding it, or rejecting it. Participate in this experience with your full body, breathing in deeply and centering yourself, allowing your thoughts to settle, and arriving fully to meet the dream.

dream diving

I call this guided meditation *dream diving*; it uses both guided imagery and active imagination. Dream diving has been helpful in bringing the dream to life in order to work with it artistically, both in dream groups I have facilitated and with individual clients. It involves diving into the dream through the imagination, bypassing the conscious mind, and welcoming spontaneous images and expressions akin to shamanic journeying and dream reentry practices. Dream diving invites intuitive insight to surface within the conscious mind through the direct experience of the imagination. This meditation arose from my own organic unconscious and seems to create a helpful, almost hypnotic framework for imaginal dialogue and active imagination. Dream diving allows the dream to arrive in real time so we have the opportunity to interact with dream images and document them in a tangible artistic form. I invite you to bring nuanced psychic material to the surface. Allow the dream to communicate through symbols, metaphors, textures, colors, and words. These impressions resonate with the deeply soulful and irrational space of the unconscious. Listen.

IMAGINAL DIALOGUE

Dreamer: Hi, my name is _____, who are you?

Dream person/energy/figure/being/image: _____

Dreamer: _____

Dream person/energy/figure/being/image: _____

_____

Dreamer: Why are you here?

Dream person/energy/figure/being/image: _____

_____

Dreamer: What do you need?

Dream person/energy/figure/being/image: _____

_____

Dreamer: _____

Dream person/energy/figure/being/image: _____

_____

Dreamer: How might I help you?

Dream person/energy/figure/being/image: _____

_____

Dreamer: How might we be in relationship or work together?

Dream person/energy/figure/being/image: _____

_____

active imagination

As I mentioned earlier, Carl Jung detailed in his writing that *active imagination* is "a sequence of fantasies produced by deliberate concentration on a particular image." A fantasy is essentially your own entertaining invention and expresses the surface of your personal desires and conscious expectations. But *active imagination*, as the term conveys, is an active process where psychic "images have a life of their own and that the symbolic events develop according to their own logic—that is, of course, if your conscious reason does not interfere. You begin by concentrating upon a starting point. But by objectifying them, the danger of their inundating consciousness is averted, and their positive effect is made accessible. It is almost impossible to find this effect in rational terms; it is a sort of 'magical' effect; that is, a suggested influence which goes out from the images to the individual, and in this way their unconscious is both extended and changed."

Jung suggested choosing a single image from a dream, vision, or picture, and introspectively observing subtle psychic changes through actively imagining. The individual perceives movement and change within their psyche during a meditation focused on the particular image, feeling, or character. Using imaginal dialogue, it is possible to deepen psychological engagement and amplify unconscious images, symbols, and figures. In using this technique along with dream diving, you will be able to follow and observe your own psychic movement and changes in real time.

IMAGINAL DIALOGUE

Dreamer: Hi, my name is _____, who are you?

Dream person/energy/figure/being/image: _____

Dreamer: _____

Dream person/energy/figure/being/image: _____

_____

Dreamer: Why are you here?

Dream person/energy/figure/being/image: _____

_____

Dreamer: What do you need?

Dream person/energy/figure/being/image: _____

_____

Dreamer: _____

Dream person/energy/figure/being/image: _____

_____

Dreamer: How might I help you?

Dream person/energy/figure/being/image: _____

_____

Dreamer: How might we be in relationship or work together?

Dream person/energy/figure/being/image: _____

_____

IMAGINAL DIALOGUE

Dreamer: Hi, my name is _____, who are you?

Dream person/energy/figure/being/image: _____

Dreamer: _____

Dream person/energy/figure/being/image: _____

_____

Dreamer: Why are you here?

Dream person/energy/figure/being/image: _____

_____

Dreamer: What do you need?

Dream person/energy/figure/being/image: _____

_____

Dreamer: _____

Dream person/energy/figure/being/image: _____

_____

Dreamer: How might I help you?

Dream person/energy/figure/being/image: _____

_____

Dreamer: How might we be in relationship or work together?

Dream person/energy/figure/being/image: _____

_____

art therapy and dreams

Art therapy involves visual expression on different levels of complexity. Art therapist Cathy Malchiodi proposed that instead of relying on cognitive functions to allocate literal interpretations when viewing artwork, an individual is able to reflect upon and respond to them on a deeper level, one that is emotional or irrational. In this way, they are listening in an equal dialogue with the conscious mind and the depths of the unconscious imagination. Expressive arts therapist and researcher Shaun McNiff pronounced, "Dreams are vital participants in our art therapy studios. Their emanation closely parallels the making of artistic images, and we respond to dreams in much the same way that we engage paintings." American art therapist Bruce Moon found that the connection between dreams and artistic images is undeniable. He stated, "Perhaps no other psychic vehicle has the power to transport people so directly into their primary needs, motivations, fears, hopes, wishes, or desires." When letting the unconscious guide, logic does not dominate this vital organic process. In fact, the brain is often more active in dreams than in waking consciousness and fosters the ability to experience wise metaphors beyond the comprehension of the logical mind; therefore, it reflects a high level of intelligence to let oneself to be informed by the unconscious.

Artistic modalities are similar to dreams, and both are a remarkable tool for accessing the unconscious mind. Through making artwork, the boundaries of the ego can dissolve, and psychic images arise. McNiff writes,

> Embracing the soul's debased expression as expressed in the images of art and dreams involves a shift in consciousness that transforms psychotherapeutic values.... [T]hey ... express an archetypal condition of soul.... [These images] may help [the artist] to accept and care for feelings of vulnerability and fragmentation that live in the shadows of the "intact" ego.

> The rejected image in a painting or dream is usually the one
> that has the most to offer.... Rather than seeing pathology in
> a painting or dream as something sick and negative, we can
> embrace it as part of the soul's nature.

Here, McNiff calls attention to the opportunity to integrate the shadow or repressed aspects of the unconscious through artwork. This attitude accepts all facets of the self and its experience that may be expressed through artistic practice.

Art therapy promotes a much deeper psychological relationship to creative work than simple elements of design and critique. It is process-oriented, focusing on the spontaneous and expressive experience in the moment and accepting the chaotic, unfinished, and unpolished visual expressions of the psyche. In fact, McNiff called art a *depth psychology* and said, "The spontaneous expressions of participants demonstrate that deep movements of psyche are made visible through paint. Art as medicine is therefore a depth psychology." Healing and therapeutic properties of art are discovered through the process of creating artwork, making it a modality of psychological inquiry that goes beyond the traditional boundaries of psychology and into the depths. Using dreams in the context of art therapy increases access to consciousness, as Moon intimated: "At no point in wakeful life are we as empowered to break through our limitations as in a dream.... They are themselves artworks, soul dramatizations that help, guide, and extend consciousness." Here, Moon implied that dreams extend conscious awareness and connect with the inner guidance of the soul.

Dreams are an autonomous and meaningful product of psychic activity, and images are the primary language of the soul. When sleeping, one is not thinking but instead is imagining. Dreams take place primarily in the right side of the brain, the hemisphere that is more spatial, kinesthetic, and pictorial. This means that the "language" of dreams is more metaphorical than discursive. Dreams do not contain symbols that can be individually interpreted, but rather present analogies that require being reexperienced holistically to be understood. Dreams are not disguised thoughts—they are simply the way that the right side of the brain "thinks." The advancement of scientific intelligence in therapeutic practice regarding the brain's hemispheres and their connections has greatly contributed to the understanding of mental images and art-making.

Images and their psychic formation, whether mental or visual, are vital in art-therapy practice because clients are able to reframe how they feel, respond to an experience, and work out feelings and thoughts on an emotional level. Unlike working with a mental image, the artwork is a tactile object that can be physically altered. Jungian analyst Joy Schaverien proclaimed, "Unlike visualization and dreams, art has a tangible and material existence. It records traces of the imaginal activity that produced it." Through art-making, an individual can actively imagine and physically express, experiment with, or depict a desired change through a collage, drawing, or painting. Hillman suggested "that we imagine a dream as a single image like a complex painting," implying that the many layers of a dream can be expressed within a single work of art. Making art can aid the client's ability to cope with stress and can be an effective tool applied under the umbrella of art therapy and in working therapeutically with dreams.

Art has historically inspired massive change socially, ideologically, and psychologically. Educators Elizabeth Thomas and Julian Rappaport highlighted the interrelationship between art and culture and discussed how art underlies and expresses political and cultural narratives. They mentioned that art has immense influence on collective identity and claimed, "What is typically thought of as 'art' is a powerful means for communicating narratives that interpret experience and shape our collective understanding of ourselves." They advised that in studying artists, "social scientists have the opportunity to . . . learn about identity development and personal and social change." In considering the power of art's role in collective change, the connection between inner work and outer transformation becomes apparent. Fostering the nonrational brilliance of the creative mind and centering within the consciousness of the dream offer an opening to return to the indigenous wisdom of many cultures. Honoring the dream's intelligence can inspire cultural development while also increasing psychological evolution in individuals.

Art as an object of psyche has power both as collective movement and within the therapeutic context. Schaverien wrote,

> Unlike visualization and dreams, art has a tangible and material existence. It records traces of the imaginal activity that produced it. Moreover, it holds, and fixes, at once moving and limiting the flow of the unconscious. In art there is a public manifestation and a shared viewing; both people see the same thing; there is an object for the shared gaze. . . . This is a significant factor within analysis because unlike other modes of active imagination the traces of its path are recorded for both people to see.

Schaverien's comment calls attention to the relationship between the art object, the psyche of the client, and that of the therapist. She stated, "The therapeutic relationship constitutes the environment within which active imagination arises. Therefore, the symbolic depth of the active imagination reflects the transference." In this way, the therapist has the opportunity to unpack the dream image. Whereas the client, as the dreamer, may have no understanding of the dream, simply the therapist's interest in the client's inner content or artwork can evoke curiosity and gratification. Embarking down this imaginal path together, both client and therapist may witness unconscious shifts. As Moon elucidated, "artworks that are based on dream images offer the art therapist a unique portal through which to connect with the inner lives of clients."

Art as therapy brings art-making beyond the cliché, bourgeois, and conceptual elitist mentality prevalent in dominant artistic culture and into the depths of the psycho-spiritual processes. I believe that the primary job of the artist initially is to get out of their own way. This means letting go of ego, control, and judgment. Doing this expands consciousness and opens the maker to creative channels, allowing them to flow through the mind and body authentically. This awareness, I believe, is a form of aesthetic intelligence. I once took a beautiful drawing class where the instructor said that art was actually a form of seeing. Drawing itself is perception and the intimate experience of witnessing; it is not about making a product. This concept changed the color of my mind forever. Art-making, as an act that happens when we are present with a dream, invites in our innate perceptions and tunes us to our immediate senses in the present moment. Don't worry about how it looks, just allow the image to arrive.

As Jung eloquently wrote, "the modern artist, after all, seeks to create art out of the unconscious. . . . The years when I was pursuing my inner images were the most important in my life." Von Franz studied more than forty thousand dreams. She determined, "The intelligence of the dream can only be compared to the other miracles of nature. . . . That is why, historically, dreams . . . have always played a role in all the various religions of the earth." This statement encompasses the true magic and wisdom that dreams offer us. Bringing dreamwork farther into the realm of mental-health culture supports humans' deepest connection to their own nature and intelligence. The noetic experience of self-discovery and collective discovery through dreams is available every night while the egoic mind is asleep. Dream therapy can be immensely healing. Jung wrote, "The avowed aim of dream-analysis is not only to exercise our wits, but to uncover and realize those hitherto unconscious contents which are considered to be of importance in the elucidation or treatment of a neurosis." Engaging dream content with consistent, creative attention and intention is a powerful tool for building a healthy relationship with the unconscious mind, hence deepening a person's relationship to their own psyche. When approached from this perspective, dreams become a genuine fountain of creative inspiration, as well as a profound tool for working through unconscious material.

It is possible to understand dreams as being presented to us as our own creative reflection. Conjuring these primordial and soulful images in the conscious state through poetry and art-making is perhaps the closest we can arrive to experiencing the waking dream. Honoring the true aliveness of dreamy psychic energy and its expression allows it to begin to move and transform. Representing these symbols in a physical way by making art brings them to life. This enables a dialogue between art and the imagination, which reveals the deep unconscious wisdom that is originally so beautifully expressed through the language of the dream.

In working through prompts in this journal, allow your dreams to metamorphosize into beautiful pieces of artwork that serve to cultivate full integration of the psychic and physical world. "A picture is an object offered for the shared gaze and therefore it may be a bridge between inner and outer, between private and public experience," said Schaverien. Your inner work becomes a transformative object of psyche and affects not only your personal growth but that of the collective. Dreamers can more wholly embrace and witness themselves in a way that includes all levels of their conscious experience, which, in turn, accelerates their psychological growth and enlightens the path of individuation. This is a space for embodiment and artistic freedom, for you to creatively engage and invite in your wildest dreams.

DREAM TITLE   DATE

I dreamed . . .

_____

_____

_____

_____

What in the dream really attracts you?

_____

_____

_____

What energy or image feels the most magnetic?

_____

_____

_____

Impressions from waking consciousness:

_____

_____

_____

_____

_____

DREAM TITLE   DATE

I dreamed . . .

_____
_____
_____
_____

What in the dream really attracts you?

_____
_____
_____

What energy or image feels the most magnetic?

_____
_____
_____

Impressions from waking consciousness:

_____
_____
_____
_____

DREAM TITLE   DATE

I dreamed . . .

_____
_____
_____
_____

What in the dream really attracts you?

_____
_____
_____

What energy or image feels the most magnetic?

_____
_____
_____

Impressions from waking consciousness:

_____
_____
_____
_____
_____

DREAM TITLE   DATE
_____   _____

I dreamed . . .
_____
_____
_____
_____
_____

What in the dream really attracts you?
_____
_____
_____
_____

What energy or image feels the most magnetic?
_____
_____
_____
_____

Impressions from waking consciousness:
_____
_____
_____
_____
_____

DREAM TITLE   DATE

I dreamed . . .

What in the dream really attracts you?

What energy or image feels the most magnetic?

Impressions from waking consciousness:

art interventions

The following are pages for drawing, collaging, or painting dream images. Here are just a few ways that you can engage with your dreams through creative expression.

COLLAGE: Collage allows us to receive the image from outside of our own conscious pressure to illustrate or create. As psychologist Jill Mellick writes in her book The Art of Dreaming, "Collage comes already half made. It meets the maker half-way across the bridge of creativity, bearing colors, forms, and texture that we only need to shape and combine." I have been making two- and three-dimensional collages since I was a young child and find a freedom and flexibility in the collage process that I have experienced with no other medium. Let colors, shapes, images, emotional content, words, and elements of design wash over your consciousness, and let your unconscious guide you.

DRAWING: Try drawing with your nondominant hand to help release the need to control your artistic process. Engage all of your senses, and note elements of the dream, such as colors, textures, shapes, sounds, smells, environment, weather, figures, objects, and such. What do you feel as you gaze at the full dream picture? What are the dream's most potent qualities? What jumps out at you? Try to stay present with your body and details of your dream experience.

PAINTING: Begin by noticing how the pigment connects with and interacts with the oil, water, or medium. Find or create a colorful hue from your dream. When you are ready to begin, place your paintbrush on the page and place your awareness on your breath. Try only moving the paintbrush across the page as you breathe. Inhale—brush stroke, exhale—brush stroke. Synchronizing your body with the act of creation allows the painting to move through you with less conscious control. Focus on how you felt in the dream, painting forms and atmospheric colors and qualities. Set your dream landscape free.

Draw, Collage, or Paint Your Dream:

Draw, Collage, or Paint Your Dream:

Draw, Collage, or Paint Your Dream:

DREAM FACTS: DID YOU KNOW?

+ Albert Einstein conceptualized his theory of relativity in a dream about cows.

+ Russian chemist Dmitri Mendeleev first classified fifty-six elements in the periodic table in a dream. They appeared to him almost entirely in the correct order after struggling for days to figure it out.

+ Danish physicist Niels Bohr conceived his depiction of the structure of an atom within a dream based on planets orbiting the sun.

+ The sewing machine was invented by Elias Howe after dreaming about cannibals trying to attack him with spears.

+ Abraham Lincoln prophesied his own assassination in a dream where he attended his own funeral.

+ Dr. James Watson conceptualized our DNA's double helix based on a dream he had about intertwining snakes.

These are just a few monumental, reality-altering, creative visions that arrived through dreams. Pay attention. Record your dreams in this journal. You never know what medicine may arrive while you sleep.

CHAPTER SEVEN

TYPES
OF DREAMS

"The doors to the world of the wild
Self are few but precious. . . . If you
love the sky and the water so much
you almost cannot bear it, that is a
door. If you yearn for a deeper life,
a full life, a sane life, that is a door."

—CLARISSA PINKOLA ESTÉS

There are many types of dreams, of which I will describe a few. Categorizing the flavors of your dreams can be a helpful practice. *Recurrent dreams* are dreams that you might have noticed recur over and over and over again throughout your life or during a particular phase or period of time. Often, they may show up again because something psychological is happening now that was also happening then, and the dreams are inviting you to make a connection between these two events or time lines. This could be a specific experience or event, or even a mental or emotional space that you are in. Dreams often recur because we have not fully processed something or have not yet received the message they are attempting to send us. They might express this message in a slightly different way in repeated dreams, or louder, or with more intensity. They are trying to get you to pay attention by bringing you the same dream over and over again if they have to.

Recurring dreams can also be an invitation to become lucid within a dream. If a dream shows up repeatedly, it could be simply that your dream-consciousness is hoping that you will recognize that you are in a dream and that you will therefore be able to become aware in your dream. You can awaken to that synchronistic, eerie, *déjà vu* moment of perception and think, "this has happened before . . . I think I had a dream of this before," and then that triggers your mind to recognize, "oh, I am dreaming." Then, you can begin to practice dreaming in a lucid state. Recurring dreams can also result from unprocessed or unresolved trauma. If you are having a dream that is traumatic or is a nightmare or a night terror that could be arising from PTSD or an actual traumatic experience, the dream could be the reexperiencing of the memory of that experience. I will discuss nightmares in more detail in the next chapter.

Prophetic, precognitive, and *prospective dreams* are dreams that overlay into the future. The difference between prophetic and prospective is that prophetic dreams depict a detailed account of something that has not yet happened, but that is going to happen in a literal sequence. A prophetic dream would be a very specific dream about something that occurs in the future, and when the event occurs, it will be exactly the way it was in the dream. A prospective dream is a little bit looser. It is more like certain elements appear in the dream that then also appear subsequently in your waking experience, but they are not necessarily bound to a particular or literal order of events in the way that a prophetic dream is. These dreams serve as possible warnings for things that are going to occur in the future, similar to a premonition or an intuition you have about a person or a place or an experience. As Jung wrote,

> Dreams prepare, announce, or warn about certain situations, often long before they actually happen. This is not necessarily a miracle or a precognition. Most crises or dangerous situations have a long incubation, only the conscious mind is not aware of it.

In some traditions, these kinds of dreams are considered "karmic" seeds that we are planting in our dream consciousness to then blossom in waking life. It is unclear whether the dream causes the events or is foreseeing the events. Because dreams are nonlinear, they are able to help us see more of our path or direction clearly. For me, prospective dreams have been really helpful along my path and individuation process.

Witnessing dreams can be lucid dreams where you remain an observer in your dream. In these dreams you are not an active participant, you are not one of the characters and you are not the main character or *dream ego*. It can feel like you are watching a movie of your own dream from above or on the sidelines. You are seeing everything occur or sometimes appear in the third person, which is where you are simultaneously a character in the dream and you are also watching yourself. These dreams are really unique, in that way where it doesn't feel as experiential, because we are observing what's happening.

Anxiety dreams arise via a myriad of factors. Disturbed sleep is clinically one of the prominent diagnostic criteria for generalized anxiety disorder. Anxiety can cause symptoms of insomnia and in turn insomnia can cause symptoms of anxiety. Often when you are anxious and hypersensitive or aware of an environment due to burnout, unprocessed grief, or depression, or just generally being an HSP (highly sensitive person) or empathic person, your boundary and your psychic space can become thin or wear out. Anxiety dreams tend to depict high action-oriented narratives with an intense emotional charge—often of fear, stress, panic, or worry. These dreams involve an experience of threat, danger, or impending harm. In my experience, when I am anxious, stressed, or experiencing burnout, my dream space becomes heightened and violently active. Finding ways to track anxiety dreams has helped me zero in on caring for my nervous system and increasing my sleep hygiene. Dreams are always pointing us toward a natural endogenous healing process: we must listen and take care of ourselves.

As discussed by Andrew Holecek, luminous dreams are metaphorically prophetic or prospective. They are some of my favorite dreams to work with, for these are dreams that portray a psychic experience that inspires our self-development. They are big dreams that foreshadow our personal, psychological, and spiritual growth, specifically how we can align ourselves with our path. Often these dreams are highly creative or vivid. You might get lots of creative ideas if you are working on a project and are unsure how it will all come together. If you do not know how to finish it, this could come to you in a dream.

Incubated dreams are intentional dreams where we send an intention or do a specific practice to incite some specific information or wisdom to come through our dreams. As discussed earlier, dream incubation rituals and rites have been practiced by cultures all over the world and for at least five thousand years. Professor Tore Nielsen writes, "Dream incubation can be understood as a form of quest to encounter a sacred being, as an attempt to bring oneself physically closer to a spiritual presence in preparation for a revelatory dream." Occult writer

Heinrich Cornelius Agrippa von Nettesheim intimated dream incubation rites in his famous *Three Books of Occult Philosophy*, noting, "... whosoever would receive divine dreams ... let him have a clean and neat chamber, also exorcized and consecrated: in the which, a perfume being made, his temples anointed ... his prayers being said, let him go to bed, earnestly meditating on that thing he desireth to know: So he shall see most true and certain dreams with the true illumination of his intellect ... he shall easily obtain the gift of oracles and dreams." You can incubate them either before bed or even in the morning or throughout your day depending on your personal practice or desired ritual. These intentionally planted seeds blossom into your dreams at night.

One caveat: I do not think it is necessarily respectful to just "big-ask" the dream, "Hey, I need this from you" out of nowhere. You should begin a practice of respectfully engaging with the dreams, because they have their own psychic life. Dreams are powerful aspects of ourselves and our consciousness that we may generally ignore, so build a relationship before you saddle them with demands.

False awakenings are dreams where you wake up in the dream from a dream. You are in a dream and then you wake up in the dream and you are still in a dream. You might be aware of this as it is happening, or you might not. This can happen many times in a dream. As a child, I called these dreams "bubble dreams," because I would blow bubbles and sometimes a bubble would get trapped inside another bubble and then the inner bubble might pop. I imagined these dreams as layers of bubbles that would sometimes pop, leaving you in the next dream. If you wake up and you are still in a dream, there are many ways to work with this experience. It may be an invitation to become lucid, or it could be a literal *awakening* that you are having in the dream, in a metaphorical or spiritual sense. I like to pay attention to dreams where there is a sudden change or shift of consciousness in the dream, even if it is just a change of scenery or environment or if you leave a place that you are in, those transitions can be important when we are participating in dreamwork.

Numinous, luminous, or *extraordinary dreams* are dreams that encompass creative, healing, parapsychological, and spiritual dreams. These dreams offer us new insight, access to wisdom, and experiences of transformation. These can be telepathic, clairvoyant, or visitation dreams, dreams where there is an astral travel or out-of-body experienced event. These dreams are undeniably powerful and magical! They show us an evolved part of ourselves, our souls, and our lives' path. These dreams often contain vivid colors, amplified feelings, strong images, meta-morphosis motifs, or animal figures. Here, we might encounter suprapersonal creative powers, deities, and qualities of the divine. These dreams can show us how to move forward along our spiritual path, resource ourselves, and creatively problem-solve.

Liminal dreams are those that often arise in hypnagogic and hypnopompic phases of sleep. Hypnagogic is the space of awareness between waking and sleep when you are falling asleep, and hypnopompic occurs between sleep and waking. These are hybrid dream-and-waking states that often include sporadic images without a narrative or immersive plot line. These dreams, like night terrors, can be non sequitur, short, thought-like, and incredibly vivid. Liminal dreams are great for zeroing in on a single impactful image or feeling, because often that is all that is present or that we remember.

Lucid dreams are dreams where the dreamer has a conscious control over what is happening within the dream. I personally believe that when we become more aware in a dream, the dream itself becomes more aware of us because we *are* the dream. Many people attempt to use lucid dreams from their dream ego's perspective, but in some ways this can be a foible; if the ego steps in forcefully or in a controlling way, it may be fun and freeing and creative or it can distract from or bypass the dream's unconscious wisdom. Even with lucid controlling dreams, there is still an active learning process occurring that is valuable. Just be careful not to get caught up in enacting your will in a space with unlimited potential.

lucid dreams in depth

LUCID DREAMING is when the dreamer becomes consciously aware that they are dreaming while staying within their dream. Making a practice of lucid dreaming can increase conscious awareness and strengthen one's ability to engage with deeper levels of the psyche, both in the personal and in the collective unconscious. As a transpersonal practice, lucid dreaming can be utilized in both therapy and within spiritual contexts such as dream yoga. I was fortunate to participate in a lucid dreaming study conducted by Denholm Aspy in 2017 that greatly amplified my dreaming practice. As a result, I had more consecutive lucid dreams than ever before. I have included some helpful tips on the following pages.

Lucid dreaming is a state that occurs during rapid eye movement (REM) sleep. REM sleep is the fifth stage of sleep, which makes up about 25 percent of your sleep cycle and first occurs about seventy to ninety minutes after you fall asleep. Because your sleep cycle repeats, you enter REM sleep several times during the night. During this state, signals are sent to the area of the part of the brain responsible for organizing information, learning, and thinking, known as the cerebral cortex, and the process of storing memories occurs. All dreams happen in this stage of sleep, but lucid dreams distinguish themselves because the lucid dreamer has conscious control and awareness, and is able to interact with the dream environment. All it takes is one moment of recognition to become lucid, though the level of lucidity often varies from barely lucid to hyper-lucid.

The benefits of lucid dreaming include lessening night terrors, building work and life skills, emotional regulation, and spiritual development. You can intentionally perform actions in lucid dreams that influence changes in fear and anxiety, especially in nightmares. Through lucidity it is possible for the dreamer to alter the story line or outcome of the nightmare. In being able to consciously interact with the nightmare, fear decreases and the rate of recurrence can become reduced.

Another potential of lucid dreaming is building work and life skills. Lucid dreaming has been used all over the world to practice difficult tasks, learn new instruments and languages, even face general fears like public speaking. Dreamwork is not only creative and spiritual, it is incredibly useful and practical. What would you like to practice in your dreams? For example, when a person is lucid-dreaming, they have access to literally any tools that might help them grow. They can practice diving, summon instruments or books, and engage in sports or other physical activities without limitation. Once a dreamer becomes experienced in inducing lucidity, they can use their ability to develop skills that are beneficial in waking life. A person is able to use the dream space to practice skills that have a direct impact on their physical muscle memory.

A study by researchers Daniel Erlacher, Tadas Stumbrys, and

Michael Schredl in 2012 showed that "9% of the lucid dreamers used this dream state to practice sport skills, and the majority of those athletes had the impression that the rehearsal within the lucid dream improved their performance in wakefulness." While the athletes cannot build muscle materially, their body memory and physiology are directly impacted. This form of rehearsal enables lucid dreamers to develop and practice tasks, all while they are asleep. This type of "mental practice is the cognitive rehearsal of a motor task in the absence of overt physical movement and in professional sport, mental rehearsal is well established."

There are also findings that the neural activities occurring during lucid dreams can increase one's ability to regulate emotions. Lucid dreaming can aid in the processing and regulating of emotions during sleep due to higher activation in the prefrontal cortex, the part of the brain in charge of emotion-regulation strategies. A study done by Kaylee Michael Ann Rosenbusch for her master's thesis at Arizona State University found that "Since lucid dreamers have higher prefrontal region activity during dreaming . . . it is clear that lucid dreaming aids in the processing of emotions during sleep." This study also provided data finding that the benefits of the stimulation of this area of the brain during sleep carries over into waking life. The brain activity present in lucid dreaming significantly increases emotional regulation skills.

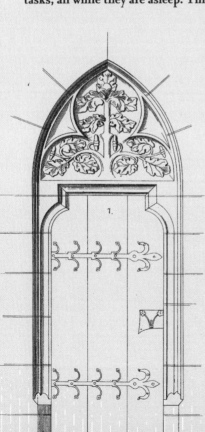

lucid dream induction

DAYTIME

Practice reality checks throughout the day so that you get in the habit; that way when you're in a dream you will be more likely to remember to do them. To do a reality check, try to push your pointer finger on your right hand through the palm of your left hand, or vice versa, depending on your personal dominance. Imagine what this might look and feel like. Obviously, when you are awake this will be impossible, but when you are dreaming your finger will usually go right through the palm of your hand. If you have a lucid dream, stay calm. Try not to get too excited, or the dream may dissolve. To stabilize the lucid state, rub your palms together and focus on the sensations in your hands. You can also caress your dream body to help solidify your dream state.

You can check to see if you are dreaming by plugging your nose, pinching it with your fingers and then trying to breathe. I find that the finger-through-the-palm is easiest. . . . Before you go to sleep, imagine what you might want to do when you become lucid—flying is a popular activity, or summoning physical representations of parts of your psyche, friends, or fantasies. Think about this possibility thoroughly and intentionally: this is a visualization practice.

Set an alarm to wake up five hours after you go to bed. Put the alarm somewhere where you must physically move to get up and turn it off. When the alarm goes off, get out of bed and turn it off. If you have to use the bathroom, do that immediately. Then get back into bed and try to remember the dream from just before you woke up. Spend a few minutes, maybe make a few notes, and remember as many details as possible. If you can't remember your dream, think of a dream you had recently and recall it in your mind. Next, lying in a comfortable position, concentrate on your intention to recognize that you are dreaming during your next dream. Repeat aloud, "Next time I'm dreaming, I will remember I'm dreaming." Put meaning and intention into the words and stay present. If your mind wanders, gently bring it back to these words. Try to stay physically still. Every time you repeat the words, imagine that you are back in the dream you just recalled and visualize yourself doing a reality test. This technique uses prospective memory, which I mentioned earlier; it can help you bring information into future conditions in order to prime your psyche for a lucid dreaming experience.

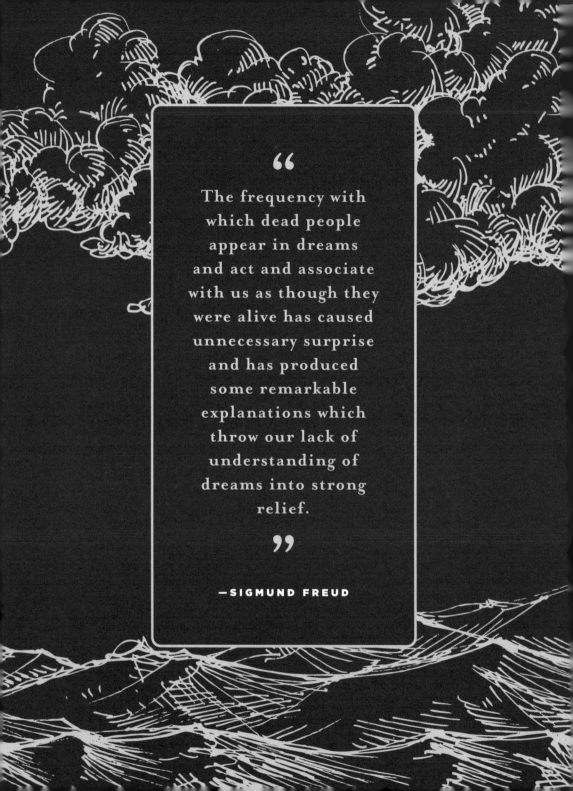

> The frequency with
> which dead people
> appear in dreams
> and act and associate
> with us as though they
> were alive has caused
> unnecessary surprise
> and has produced
> some remarkable
> explanations which
> throw our lack of
> understanding of
> dreams into strong
> relief.

—SIGMUND FREUD

nighttime visitations and nocturnal mediations

The sections below touch on aspects of liminal space and the practice of dream yoga.

nighttime visitors

Our ancestors, loved ones, and spirits that have passed can often visit us in our dream space. When these figures show up, there is a palpable energetic shift within the dream. It can sometimes be difficult to discern, but you will know the difference between a real visitor from beyond and a piece of your own psyche expressing itself through the cloak of the dead. (Although the dream might enact an ancient familial memory or take place in the realm of the dead.) Usually, if you are visited by a relative or ghost figure from beyond the veil, they will not be integrated into the narrative of your dream. Likely, ancestral figures and guides will show up separately and of their own accord, and this part of the dream will stick out from the rest. For example, they might appear out of nowhere, enter and leave quickly, or be surrounded by a gaping hole in space. They might speak directly to you or give you a knowing glance; you can feel the difference. Through conscious dreaming, we might develop a talent for discussion with the departed within the dream space.

Have you ever been visited? Describe your experience below:

Ancient Buddhist practitioners have used nocturnal meditations and dream yoga as a spiritual practice, and even as preparation for death. I was fortunate enough to attend one of educator and author Andrew Holecek's Dream Yoga retreats as an undergraduate psychology student conducting research for Naropa University's Cognitive and Affective Science Lab. While my personal path is oriented in esoteric Judaism, I have learned an immense amount about dreaming and consciousness from a Buddhist perspective. In sharing here about dream yoga, my intention is to educate and inspire your continued curiosity concerning the diverse ways of engaging with dreams and their legacy of practices. These traditions are far older than Western science, and their magic is compelling to consider.

Dream yoga often begins with lucid dreaming, where you become fully conscious within your dream ego inside of the dream. Here, you can interact with pieces of yourself within the dream, and even energies and entities beyond it. The transformative potential of dreams is valued in Tibetan culture, and within Tibetan Buddhism there is a type of dreams called "Milam Ter," which translates as *dream treasure*. For more than a thousand years, Tibetan Buddhists have believed that it is possible to be just as aware during dream state as we are during waking state. Their ritual practice of this, dream yoga, proposes exercises that can be used in waking state and within lucid dreams to facilitate spiritual awakening and enlightenment. The oldest teaching on dream yoga is titled "The Six Doctrines" or "Yogas of Naropa." Dream yoga is based on a three-tiered model of consciousness, which includes psyche, substrate, and the primordial clear-light mind. It is considered to be an advanced practice for individuals who have already developed a relatively stable mind and are familiar with yogic and meditation practices. The stability and clarity of your dreams can reflect the stability and clarity of your mind and attention.

Dream yoga is a complete spiritual path, designed to allow you to discover and rest in the clear-light mind, which is the fundamentally ineffable, deepest

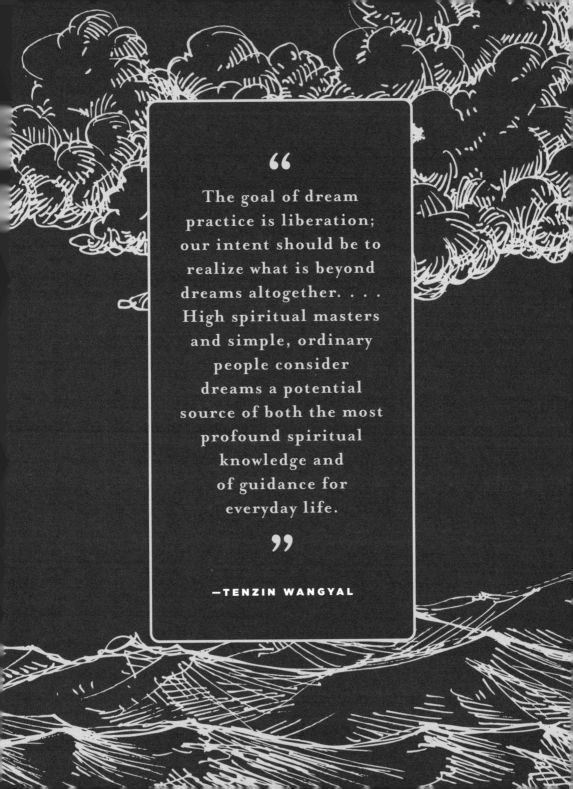

> The goal of dream practice is liberation; our intent should be to realize what is beyond dreams altogether. . . . High spiritual masters and simple, ordinary people consider dreams a potential source of both the most profound spiritual knowledge and of guidance for everyday life.
>
> —TENZIN WANGYAL

level of mind, below psyche and substrate consciousness. The clear-light mind never sleeps and is considered by Tibetan Buddhists to exist in our deepest sleep. It is the innate enlightened mind. This means that the awakened and lucid state is our natural, most basic state of mind. Dream Yoga simply utilizes lucidity and night practices to remove obstructions that exist in the relative mind, the psyche and the substrate unconscious. Mindfulness is essentially the practice of lucidity, as by being mindful we are actually "waking up," as in *awakening*, to the present moment, as Holecek describes. This clarity and awakeness is analogous to lucidity. When we say "thinking" in meditation, we actually mean "wake up"—it is a call to beingness from our witnessing consciousness. Dream yogis consider waking life to be the state of being asleep and see no difference between the illusion of reality in either waking or dream states. *Samsaric*, beings stuck in their karmic patterns, are known as sleepwalkers. This language conveys the flexibility understood when perceiving the waking and sleeping states. By becoming lucid, one can be able to mindfully work through karma within a dream, which is an opportunity to potentially break karmic patterns on a deeper psychic level. All sleep, day and night, is ignorance of our primordial awakened state.

There are three primary stages of dream yoga, and within these three stages there are nine secondary stages. The first primary stage is recognition of "the nature of the dream state." This stage involves the preliminary awareness of recognizing that the dream is in fact a dream. Once one is well versed in their own dream language, they can begin employing the first secondary stage, which is using "state checks" to trigger lucidity within a dream. This instruction states that when one becomes aware that one is dreaming, one becomes lucid and should fly around playfully engaging with the dream. There are many ways to trigger lucidity; one of my personal favorites, as mentioned prior, is to try to put your pointer finger through your opposite hand throughout the day. If you do this consistently, chances are that when you are within a dream you will remember to do it, and your pointer finger will go straight through your hand. This will trigger your mind to let you know that you are dreaming, and from there you can become lucid.

In the practice of dream yoga, you can meditate within a dream and purposely conjure experiences and transformative actions to help evolve your consciousness. Your inner world of awareness is a great place to work with fear and shadow figures. You can go even deeper there than in the waking world—once conscious within a dream, you can travel below the threshold of awareness into dreamless sleep. This is the nondualistic state of emptiness where time and space do not exist, and there it is possible to access information, wisdom, and spiritual teachers from across time lines.

In dream yoga, sleeping is likened to a daily death, and this becomes a practice for the death that occurs at the end of life. Each night, we pass from consciousness into unconsciousness, where we are we born into the dream; this mirrors the Buddhist perspective of the dying process. If we become more conscious in our dreams, then we can potentially become more conscious beyond death. This deep inner practice is as beautiful as it is difficult, accessible to every sleeping mind that wishes to awaken within a dream.

CHAPTER EIGHT

NIGHTMARES

Nightmares, ominous and full of shadow figures that seem ripe with menace, are, in fact, conduits of potent energy. They show us where we are intrapsychically, meaning internally psychologically bound, and have no problem presenting us with the things we wish to avoid most, especially in dreams.

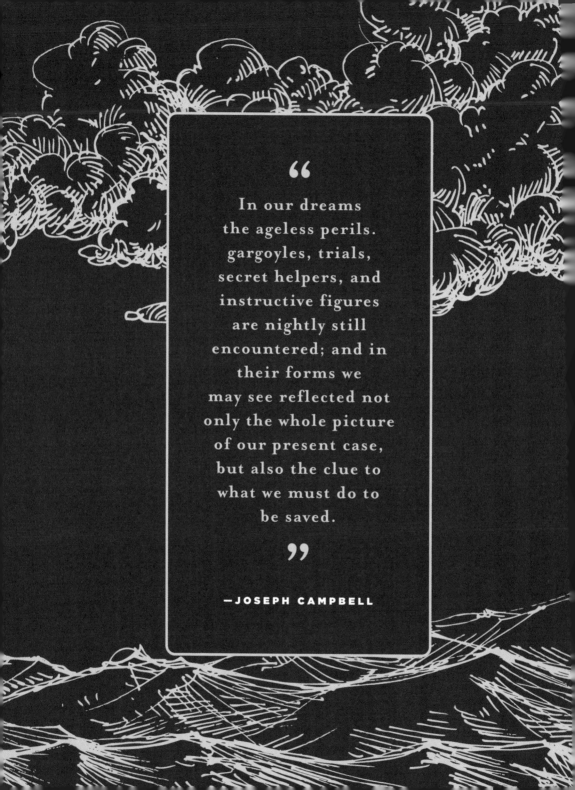

> "
>
> In our dreams
> the ageless perils.
> gargoyles, trials,
> secret helpers, and
> instructive figures
> are nightly still
> encountered; and in
> their forms we
> may see reflected not
> only the whole picture
> of our present case,
> but also the clue to
> what we must do to
> be saved.
>
> "

—JOSEPH CAMPBELL

Our shadow can appear in nightmares as perils, gargoyles, tricksters, unsightly beings, or maybe just someone we don't like. These figures are often helpful guideposts at a crossroads showing us exactly which way we need to go. When we can address and face these rejected parts of our psyche, we can further integrate our wholeness and take back our personal power.

This section is an amalgamation of the following topics: transitional experiences, which includes hypnogogia, hypnopompia, sleep paralysis, and nightmares. I wanted to include these topics from a general neurobiological perspective, because I think it can be helpful to have a manual for our physical vessel and an understanding of the dynamics that are occurring within us and how they affect our shadow work and nightmare experiences.

As I mentioned earlier, every night we go through several different types of sleep or sleep stages, and most of our dreams occur during the stage of rapid eye movement (REM) sleep. I chose to include and address sleep paralysis because over the years I have received quite a few questions around this topic, including people reaching out and sharing their frightening experiences. I want to ground this in a scientific perspective and present this information so that maybe it can help people who experience sleep paralysis. Despite being so active in dreaming during REM sleep, our bodies are largely paralyzed. All muscles—with the exceptions of the muscles in the eye, the diaphragm, and the sphincters at the top and bottom of the gastrointestinal tract—develop complete weakness. ALL of our other muscles. So, all these muscles are essentially shut down while we are asleep. When our body goes into this paralysis, we are literally sending the exact same signals to our biophysiological system as when we are consciously awake. During REM sleep, our voluntary muscles become temporary disabled so that we do not actually act out our dreams in waking life. As you can imagine, that could be very destructive and harmful. If we climbed a mountain in our dream, and then also did that in our waking life, we might end up accidentally jumping out a window and hurting our bodies, our possessions, or our home.

Sleep paralysis generally involves being conscious and aware of the room around you while being unable to move or speak, often accompanied by vivid auditory and visual hallucinations, which evidently result from the same processes that produce dreams during REM sleep. It is not unusual to have the vivid visual hallucinations during sleep paralysis. These are usually called "hypnopompic hallucinations." Sleep paralysis can be understood as a state of both being awake and dreaming. Depth psychology scholars Oreet Rees and Leanne Whitney explain, "The sleep paralysis nightmare has been reported from antiquity to modernity across manifold cultures. Many people who experience nocturnal assaults by dark entities, demons, hags, or incubi during sleep paralysis ascribe them to evil spirits with varying degrees of malevolence. The majority report the episodes as terrifying, mysterious, and uncanny." Known in the neurocognitive literature as "isolated sleep paralysis" or "sleep paralysis with hypnagogic and hypnopompic hallucinations," the phenomenon is fascinating to researchers across disciplines because it occurs when we are both asleep and awake, presenting fundamental questions about conscious experiences in sleep. At the same time, people can become quite frightened or seriously paralyzed, especially if they are unaware of what is happening to them. Unusual physical sensations like tingling, floating, and difficulty breathing are also sometimes reported. This feels frightening, but it is otherwise not usually harmful.

Sleep paralysis is common and occurs naturally. An estimated 20 to 60 percent of the human population experiences sleep paralysis at least once in their lives. You may have already experienced it. And although it can be scary, it is important to remember that it poses no medical risk. It almost always lasts only for a few minutes, sometimes a matter of seconds. It can happen generally at two different times during the sleep cycle, while you are waking up during the hypnopompic phase and also while you are falling asleep during the hypnagogic phase. So, if you are falling asleep and your mind remains heightened or active, sometimes you will go into sleep paralysis or have hypnogogic hallucinations. This can also happen during the hypnopompic phase when you are waking up. The hypnopompic phase is actually the most common period in which people experience sleep paralysis.

One of the best strategies to avoid sleep paralysis that you can do is create healthy sleeping habits. Try to get at least eight hours every night and have a regular sleep cycle with no disruptions. (Refer back to sleep hygiene and rituals.) If you do experience sleep paralysis, there are several things that you can do to make this less frightening and to help it end quickly. The most important thing to do is not to panic. Make sure that you do not struggle to move your body, as this can actually prolong your experience of sleep paralysis. Remember that sleep paralysis is totally harmless. Try repeating to yourself: "This is harmless and it will soon end; this is harmless and it will soon be over. It will not take long." Breathing in a controlled manner can help you stay calm, so try to make your breathing slow and deep, taking maybe five seconds to inhale and five to seven seconds to exhale. In through the nose and out through the mouth. This helps activate the parasympathetic nervous system, calm you down, and help expand the diaphragm (which is not paralyzed) to help the experience end more quickly.

If you can relax, you can also try making small movements with your fingers and toes. These parts of the body can be less paralyzed, so moving them can actually initiate you freeing up the rest of the muscles of your body. If this doesn't work, try coughing or intense breathing to activate the muscles in your diaphragm. Sometimes coughing or intense breathing can snap you out of sleep. Much of this information comes from a study done by Denholm Aspy, who is a psychologist in Australia who studies lucid dreams. I've included citations in the resources section at the end of this book if you want to go more deeply into the topics of sleep paralysis, entities, and common mythological hypnopompic hallucinations.

Draw your sleep paralysis visitors or hypnopompic images:

In investigating our nightmarish figures that appear in dreams and during sleep paralysis, sometimes an apparition comes not just to be scary, but to be heard. Going through the following are some common figures that appear during sleep paralysis.

One figure that you might see during sleep paralysis is a small person, maybe appearing to you as a brownie, fairy, goblin, or dark elf. These are mischievous beings that may come to you during sleep paralysis visions. In German, the word nightmare, albtraum, literally means bad dream caused by an elf sitting on your chest. These entities can be playful, although they are not pleasant to look at. Traditionally, brownies are blamed for lost objects and often poltergeist activity in homes. They may tease you or poke you while you are asleep.

Often in sleep paralysis, there is the experience of a dark or hooded figure putting pressure on one's chest. In medieval Europe, accounts suggested that demons would sit on the sufferer's chest and sexually aggress them against their will. These demons were known in the masculine form as the incubus and in the feminine form as the succubus. These encounters are still present today, and they can often look like entities who are partially dead or half human and try to have sex with the person who is sleeping. Many people are haunted by the dead during sleep. Often, this occurs where the witness, who is lying in bed awake and in sleep paralysis, suddenly feels a presence in the room. An apparition may then come sit on the bed, or appear as a set of ghostly hands. Dead people show up all the time. It is common to see them standing by the side of the bed, unable to speak. The silent entities can sometimes communicate with intentional thoughts, so it's possible to ask the figure "What do you want?" or "Who are you?"

According to Ryan Hurd, the author of Sleep Paralysis, the literature on the connection between hypnagogic hallucinations and psychic effects is vast and comes with many parallel threads. Telepathy, ESP, and mutual dreams have been cited in religious contexts and in accounts through occult texts and modern controlled studies in general dream research. In looking at this aspect of dreaming, the research suggests that occurrences of hypnagogia, hypnopompia, and sleep paralysis may be more conducive to these forms of subtle and paranormal communication, specifically telepathy. This is why it might be beneficial to speak even though you cannot move your mouth, with your thoughts turned intentionally to the apparitions that are in the room with you during sleep paralysis.

Ryan Hurd also discusses *allies, angels,* and *aliens.* There are many interdimensional figures, figments of our imagination, and fantasy and dream characters that can appear to us through hypnopompic hallucinations. During sleep paralysis, these figures might have glowing eyes or be reminiscent of mythological figures or various cultures throughout time, embodying archetypes, such as the black dog or aliens, or a true religious or mystical experience with angels or archangels.

These figures could be part of your own psyche or the collective. If you experience a sleep paralysis figure or apparition, record it in your dream journal and write down what it looks like, describing its color, texture, shape, and essence. Make note if it communicated with you.

nightmares

Nightmares are a form of parasomnia, which occur often with an average of one to two weekly in 10 percent of the population. Why do we have nightmares? There are many reasons ranging from the biological to the spiritual. There are many current scientific theories concerning why we experience REM sleep in general or have dreams. One of which is that it allows us to rehearse instinctive behaviors that are critical to our survival. Others suggest that it somehow prepares certain circuits of the brain for daily functions and activities. Dreams have also been shown to affect mood regulation and psychological state. Good sleep can result in marked improvement in mood and overall physiological health. According to integrative neurologist and sleep specialist Smita Patel, sleeping can be said to scrub away the brain plaque or accumulated waste metabolites and proteins

Draw your sleep paralysis visitors or hypnopompic images:

that we amass that have been shown to lead to cognitive decline and Alzheimer's disease. Sleeping is healthy! But what about nightmares?

Many neurobiological models consider nightmares to be mood regulators, priming us for possible threats. If we experience something intense in a dream and then it occurs in our waking life, we are already ready to respond to the situation. Sleep terrors, which are not nightmares, are often common in children and occur when a child screams and cries inconsolably in the middle of the night and then goes back to sleep, subsequently not remembering any of their nighttime experience. They have no recollection of what happened to them. This condition is a non-REM parasomnia and arises during very deep non-REM, nondreaming sleep. Sleep walking is also a non-REM parasomnia, which means that when someone is sleepwalking, it is not likely that they're in a nightmare or a full-fledged dream.

In sleepwalking or sleep terrors, the experience is usually visual or emotional imagery of a disjointed nature. That could manifest as a non sequitur occurrence of a simple color, shape, or emotion, or an intense experience like walls crashing down, or just an abyss. It will be something that isn't connected to a larger story or narrative. Sleep has actually been found to be a local occurrence in the brain, which means that sleep does not affect the brain as a whole. This is really fascinating to me. Different parts of the brain can be simultaneously in different states of wakefulness or sleep. Animals also experience similar sleeping patterns, such as what is termed "uni-hemispheric sleep." This is how aquatic mammals swim and surface to breathe while they're asleep. In the same way, many birds are able to continue to fly while they are asleep.

Nightmares and sleep terrors are often a symptom of PTSD or a traumatic event, recurring nightmares that begin after trauma and persist for more than a month or even over the years. This can include a reexperiencing of the traumatic event that occurred, which might be a scene replayed over and over that contains specifics to the trauma. To the person experiencing a nightmare, that literal reenactment of a traumatic event can be a type of emotional processing that happens while we are asleep. This means that working within the nightmare itself is going to bring up deep work that might best be held and aided in a therapeutic setting. Reactivating trauma can retraumatize a person or continue to cause further distress in these cases. Therapy can be extremely helpful, especially the use of EMDR (eye movement desensitization reprocessing). This helps recontextualize the trauma, freeing it from being trapped in the amygdala, which governs our fear responses, to creating a safe space for the memory to be integrated into the hippocampus so that it doesn't continue to cause hyperarousal. Using the repeated experiencing of the trauma, EMDR therapy is an integrative psycho-therapeutic approach that has been extensively researched and proven effective for the treatment of trauma using eye movements or other bilateral stimulations. Often lights or tapping or buttons are used to access the same part of the unconscious process that occurs in REM sleep. The therapist facilitates the accessing of the traumatic memory network, so that new associations begin to forge between the traumatic memory and more adaptive memories. This informs the approach that we use when working with our own nightmares; and within a guided clinical setting. Nightmares, from a Jungian perspective, that are not related to specific trauma can serve to bring unconscious material directly to the surface of consciousness.

Nightmares are not necessarily an indication that something is wrong. They are often more effective messengers. We often remember nightmares more than we do other types of dreams because they are so visually and emotionally impactful. This is for a number of reasons, one being that nightmares are specifically formulated to get your attention. A nightmare figure may have something important to communicate to you or be an aspect of your psyche or shadow that is starved for nourishment and attention. I really like this example: When you receive a phone call from someone you love, you trust the source and you instantly pick up or respond. A nightmare has a bad reputation for being a frightening message. And most people avoid, suppress, repress, or run from them. But even when the communication is scary, if you can let go of your preconceptions and welcome nightmares as a conversation you want to have with a wiser part of yourself, a recurring nightmare can be similar to an exclamation point. It is saying "Pay attention. You have to deal with this. You have to hear me. You have to listen to me. You have to see me as having an urgent message that does not get through or is repressed."

Nightmares can become more and more extreme. For example, the guns might get larger, or the explosions louder and more intense. The dream characters may become more and more violent until the intensity becomes unbearable and its extreme nature finally gets your attention. So, I have people ask me, "I have this nightmare. It keeps returning; it won't go away. How do I make it go away?" The answer is, if you are suppressing it or repressing it or ignoring it, it will not go away. It will just get bigger, stronger, and louder. When a nightmare wakes you up, you can feel terrified, raw, and intense for hours, even unhinged. A nightmare about a physical symptom could inspire you to check out a health issue. A nightmare about a car crash could suggest that you need to stop fighting the inevitable crash of a relationship, spiritual direction, or vocational shift. Imagine viewing it symbolically and without fear to approach its message.

However, nightmares can be true, literal warnings. And while the nightmare may warn you, you might still need to decipher what the challenges are and how to deal with them. Sometimes a warning dream can help you avoid the worst, and sometimes it can just prepare you for what is going to come. Author Stase Michaels wrote that, like a yellow traffic signal, a warning nightmare screams "Put the brakes on, stay alert, assess what you see as you go forward!" Are you going to crash? YOU know, this is a symbol that is coming through your own individual unconscious to communicate something to you.

Nightmares are not necessarily an indication that something is wrong emotionally or psychologically; this is generally a misconception. Although, they can be an indication of nervous system dysregulation, adrenal fatigue, or an overload of toxic stress. If you have a history of complex trauma, post-traumatic stress, or hypervigilance, be mindful to support your inner work through nervous system regulation and trauma healing. If this is the case for you, notice how your nightmare patterns relate to your embodied experience or psychological stress and take care of yourself. See a therapist, take a bath, and, above all, REST. If the dream is operating symbolically, pay attention to how you felt in the dream. Nightmares are often more effective psychic messengers, because, while our ego and our conscious mind delineate things like good and bad, our unconscious mind doesn't have any such delineation. Dreams are amoral. A nightmare therefore could be a horrific event, which your unconscious perceives as a creative expression of some message that it's trying to send to you. You can begin to think of nightmare characters as representations of parts of your inner personalities. They may just want to be invited or included. They can become distressed or act out in the same way that many people do when they feel unloved or disconnected. Using this model, it can be helpful to consider an outcasted or an uncomfortable nightmare or a shadow figure as a good object for a meditative practice, such as guided imagery or active imagination.

The word *demon* originates from the Greek word *daemon* or *daimon*, which is described as a person's genius, divine power, or guiding spirit. With the influence of Christianity appropriating earlier pagan beliefs, the word took on a reputation as evil. By attending to our demons, they can be changed and returned to their powerful roles as our allies: our daimons. Through nourishing our demons, we can nurture and transform these energies, giving them a home and purpose within us. Take a moment to consider a demon or nightmare figure that shows up for you—not the most horrifying or dangerous one, but perhaps one that follows you around daily, inhibiting your true authentic self-expression, or one that shows up in your dreams, forgotten or forlorn. If you consider the demon that arises for you, rate it in terms of "threatening," "dangerous," and "terrifying." For this experiential practice we are going to be working with demons/shadow figures that are less scary. You might even use an element of your "golden" shadow, as previously described. As with all psychic work, it is important to begin to integrate slowly, so that the personality can appropriately adjust and integrate, without splintering. As you continue to practice this work, you may consider inviting more menacing demons into your space, but it is important to begin small, especially if you have very thin psychic boundaries or an unstable ego.

a guided experience for working with nightmares and the shadow

To prepare for this exercise and guided experience, you will need a notebook and writing utensil, and two chairs facing each other: one for yourself and one for your shadow aspect or nightmare demon. Make sure that you are in a safe space, that you have a glass of water, and that you are conscious of the fact that you have the ability to stop at any time if your experience becomes overwhelming. It can help to let a trusted friend know you are embarking upon this journey and ask for them to check in with you afterward or be available if you need support or coregulation. This is also an activity you might do with your therapist as your guide.

Before you begin, find a comfortable seated position, place the soles of your feet firmly on the ground, and rest your hands gently by your sides or on the tops of your thighs. Close your eyes and begin to relax. You will be entering the space of the unconscious imaginal world. If you can, keep your eyes closed throughout the duration of this experience.

Take a deep breath, breathing all the way down into your diaphragm and exhaling slowly through your nostrils.

Inhale, noticing where you may feel tension throughout your body.

Send your breath toward these tight spaces, opening and releasing the tension with the out breath.

Again, inhale slowly, bringing oxygen into any physical tension in the body.

Exhale, releasing the last breath outward.

Notice how you are feeling in your body, in your mind, in your spirit.

Next, breathe into any emotions you may be carrying from earlier in your day. Notice what arises in your feeling space and any resistance or constriction. Inhale, bringing your breath through those feelings and dispersing them outward with your exhalation.

Slowly inhaling, notice any emotion that appears and surround it with your calm, spacious breath. Lastly, take a deep breath toward any thoughts that are persistent. Pulling your rhythmic breathing toward your mind, comb through any stress or worries with the expanse of oxygen.

Observe what thoughts you're holding in your body, in your heart, and in your mind, bringing your relaxed breath toward those tensions and unwinding them with your final exhalation.

Once you feel centered, consider why you have invoked this practice.

What is your intention? Be clear.

Look inward first. Find the shadow or nightmare demon within your body.

Which demon arises?

Which demon would you like to work with?

Where does it live within you?

If it surfaced in a nightmare, where were you?

Begin to bring the memory back so that you can feel the demon strongly or visualize it clearly.

If you had an experience that activated your shadow, what was it?

Staying connected to your body, notice where you feel the demon residing. You can start to feel where it is held within you. Keeping your eyes closed and continuing to breathe, just begin to observe.

What shape is the demon?

What color or colors does it display?

Looking closer, what texture is it?

Slowly bring the demon into focus. Begin to notice. Consider this figure's temperature; is this demon cold-blooded? Or perhaps flaming hot?

Does it make any noticeable sounds or movements?

Bring the energy toward you and gently intensify it.

When you can see the demon clearly inside yourself, allow the sensation—including the colors, texture, temperature, and anything else that you observed—to slowly move out of your body and become a being with limbs, a face, and eyes.

If it feels more abstract, like a concept, what might you imagine it to look like? If this demon were to become a being, personify it. Notice it's standing up right in front of you. It walks over and seats itself in the chair across from you. You are now facing the shadow aspect or demon. With your eyes still closed, notice how it looks curiously at you from the adjacent chair. Notice how big or how small it might be.

What size is it?

What does its skin or surface look like? Be curious.

What color is it?

How is the demon feeling?

What do you notice?

Is there anything new or surprising showing up that you did not see before?

How about now?

Just take a moment to talk with the demon or nightmare figure.

Dreamer: Hi, my name is _____, who are you?

Dream person/energy/figure/being/image: _____

You: _____

Shadow person/energy/figure/being/image: _____

You: Why are you here?

Shadow person/energy/figure/being/image: _____

You: What do you need?

Shadow person/energy/figure/being/image: _____

Take a moment here to look down, in your mind's eye, at your hands; in them is a gift or offering for your shadow figure. What is it?

Offer this to them and notice their response; are they able to receive it? How do they shift or change when you offer them this gift?

Shadow person/energy/figure/being/image: _____

You: How might I help you?

Shadow person/energy/figure/being/image: _____

You: How might we be in relationship or work together?

Shadow person/energy/figure/being/image: _____

Now, as you gradually begin to softly and slowly open your eyes, hold the feeling of the energy of the experience within your body, reach for your journal close by, and begin to record and reflect upon this experience. Remember what happened. Think about the interaction.

What came up for you within yourself?

_____

_____

What happened?

_____

_____

What did you see?

_____

_____

What did you notice?

_____

_____

What did you learn and how do you feel?

_____

_____

Take a few minutes to journal about this experience, and be curious about the transformation that may have occurred.

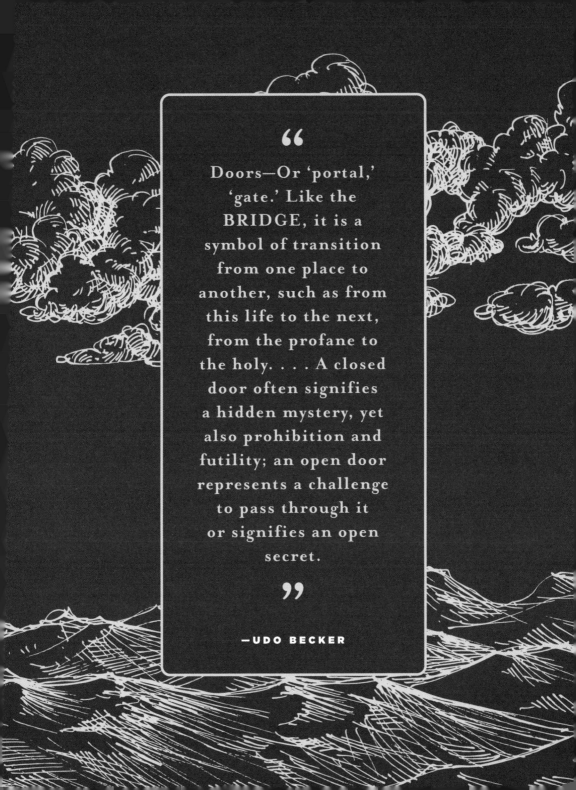

> **"**
>
> Doors—Or 'portal,' 'gate.' Like the BRIDGE, it is a symbol of transition from one place to another, such as from this life to the next, from the profane to the holy. . . . A closed door often signifies a hidden mystery, yet also prohibition and futility; an open door represents a challenge to pass through it or signifies an open secret.
>
> **"**
>
> —UDO BECKER

LOOKING BACK THROUGH THE DOOR

How do you feel, having opened the little hidden doors of your dreams? As you have witnessed, there are many ways to engage with dreams, and every person has the capacity to explore what works for their unique dreaming mind and personal process. Many people have dreams, whether they want to or not, and most will have dreams until the day they die. This psycho-spiritual work is accessible every night during sleep to almost everyone, and dream life is a part of our existence, continually showing up and asking to be explored. It is the least we can do to answer the call, in what way feels right, at the time that we are ready. It cannot be denied that humans across history have derived immeasurable benefits from dreamwork. Instead of privileging waking consciousness, it may be helpful to consider being more accountable to the dream. Because consciousness extends beyond what we are aware of to include the entire unconscious mind, we give space for this unconsciousness to come forward and be made conscious when we attend to the images presented in dreams.

Truly the most consistent, available, and creative nonordinary state of consciousness humans experience is that of the dream. Dreams are portals of the deep and the divine, the mythopoesis of the soul. They are elaborately dressed images and symbols packed with potent psychic energy that express the deeper aspects of ourselves, dancing while we slumber. Learning to engage with dreams changes the way we perceive the world. When we learn to see these nightly treasures as beautiful imaginal metaphors full of psychic material, we begin to integrate the wisdom of the dreaming mind. Dreams emulate flow states ideal for creativity and healing and can be likened easily to artwork, stories, myths, and films. They contain costumed figures, heroic journeys, fantastical landscapes, and powerful emotional experiences.

As occult author Peter Grey discussed, "The diving bell of psychoanalysis has been hauled to the surface, trespassing as it did in the world of magic, and dream has once more been marginalised and mocked as insubstantial. We need to lend it massy weight. Our conception of dreams needs healing before we can in turn be healed by them. There is no price which can be placed upon this." Echoing the deep importance of our dreams and how they usher us into our priceless magical inner space, this reclamation is primary in our return to a soulful and animated world. Grey wrote, "The dream diary is a practice to cultivate, or our dreams fall away forgotten. This connects us to a ritual continuum. . . . We must learn to extend our control, not allow others to descend for us and peer out through thick glass, but plunge in ourselves as naked as pearl divers and return with the treasures of the undersea garden." His poetic words suggest that this work can only be done by us, that it is our birthright to dive into our dreams and retrieve the pearls of wisdom harbored in the flowering bed of the oceanic unconscious. Living a symbolic life is truly the greatest gift.

As a blossoming psychotherapist, the Jungian, post-Jungian, and ancient mystical theoretical frameworks serve as useful apparatus for integrating dreams into waking consciousness in service of psychological and spiritual growth. Furthering my own knowledge and experience with dreams, myths, and archetypes has fostered my development of a vibrant, depth-oriented therapeutic style to engage deeply with my client's unconscious. It has changed my psyche forever, and the thousands of hours that I spend with the psyches of others continue to reveal depths of metamorphosis through dreamwork that I never knew was possible. Excavating, pruning, and planting, we tend to the ecology of deep psyche, fostering dreams that show us what is beyond conscious conception. This is how we change the world from the inside out.

Whether you create a dream altar or consider less screen time before bed, I hope the synthesis of information and experiences presented in this book inspires you to go deeper. Here I offer you over a decade of research and experience to scaffold an inner working that can transform your life. From the scientific to the psychological to the spiritual, dreams offer us multidimensional knowledge to bring into our waking lives for healing. As you embark upon your dreamwork journey through art, writing, listening, imagination, and psychotherapy, I hope you notice the continual return to yourself, to your unique and rich process of individuation, and a lifetime of inner transformation.

Follow your dreams into the depths and learn to perceive them as vivid visual gifts that can enable your psyche to fully realize and express itself. You don't have to be an artist to begin to unveil and converse with the compelling images of your deep psyche. Allow these myths, paintings, doodles, images, feelings, and symbols to arise and lead you toward self-actualization and meaningful connection. Arising from the depths of the psychic, union dreams unite us with our wholeness, our humaness, and the infinite constellation of divine creative forces. Dreams are powerful messengers pulling our consciousness forward into the collective growth and healing that we all desire, so we can artfully create a new paradigm together. Deep dreamer, you are the key. Bring back these remnants of primordial truth; this world needs your magic.

RESOURCES

about this book

Jung, Carl Gustav. (1970). "Civilization in transition (CW, Vol. 10)." In The Symbolic Life, Second Edition, Routledge. (Original work published 1964).

Ogden, Thomas H. (2007) This Art of Psychoanalysis: Dreaming Undreamt Dreams and Interrupted Cries. Routledge.

preface. through dreams i arrived . . .

ArtHearty. (n.d.). Exploring the Deep Connection Between Art and Spirituality. https://arthearty.com/exploring -connection-between-art-spirituality.

Dyrness, William A. (2001). Visual Faith: Art, Theology, and Worship in Dialogue. Baker Academic.

Elgood, Heather. (2000) Hinduism and the Religious Arts. A&C Black.

Dissanayake, Ellen. (1990). What Is Art for? University of Washington Press.

Hobson, John Allan. (1988). The Dreaming Brain. Basic Books.

Holecek, Andrew. (2016). Dream Yoga: Illuminating Your Life Through Lucid Dreaming and the Tibetan Yogas of Sleep. Sounds True.

Jung, Carl Gustav. (1967). The Collected Works of C. G. Jung: Vol. 5. Symbols of Transformation (R. F. C. Hull, Trans.) (H. Read et al., Eds.). Princeton University Press. (Original work published 1952.)

Moss, Robert. (2010) Conscious Dreaming: A Spiritual Path for Everyday Life. Harmony.

Naiman, Rubin. (2021). "Integrative Dream Medicine." In Valerie Cacho & Esther Lum (Eds.), Integrative Sleep Medicine. Oxford University Press.

Sharp, Daryl. (1991). C. G. Jung Lexicon: A Primer of Terms and Concepts. Inner City Books.

Shulman, David, & Stroumsa, Guy G. (1999). "Introduction." In D. Shulman & G. G. Stroumsa (Eds.), Dream Cultures: Explorations in the Comparative History of Dreaming. Oxford University Press.

1. introduction

Bulkeley, Kelly. (2016) Big Dreams: The Science of Dreaming and the Origins of Religion. Oxford University Press.

Calkins, Mary Whiton. (1893). "Statistics of Dreams." The American Journal of Psychology, 5, no. 3.

Dement, William. (1960). "The Effect of Dream Deprivation: The need for a certain amount of dreaming each night is suggested by recent experiments." Science, 131, no. 3415

Hobson, John Allan. (1988). The Dreaming Brain. Basic Books.

Jung, Carl Gustav. (2014). Collected Works of C. G. Jung, Volume 10: Civilization in Transition (Vol. 49). Princeton University Press. Para 305.

Naiman, Rubin. (2021). "Integrative Dream Medicine." In Valerie Cacho & Esther Lum (Eds.), Integrative Sleep Medicine. Oxford University Press.

2. remembering and recording dreams

Betz, Hans Dieter. (Ed.). (2022). The Greek Magical Papyri in Translation, Including the Demotic Spells, Volume 1. University of Chicago Press.

Faraone, Christopher A. (2020). "The Use of Divine Images in the Dream—Divination Recipes of the Greek Magical Papyri." In Attilio Mastrocinque, Joseph E. Sanzo, and Marianna Scapini (Eds.), Ancient Magic: Then and Now. Franz Steiner Verlag Wiesbaden GmbH.

Jung, Carl Gustav. (2014). Collected Works of C. G. Jung, Volume 10: Civilization in Transition (Vol. 49). Princeton University Press.

Neos Alexandria. https://neosalexandria.org/the -pantheon/bes/excerpt-from-british-museum-papyrus -122/.

Ochs, Vanessa L., & Ochs, Elizabeth. (2003). The Jewish Dream Book: The Key to Opening the Inner Meaning of Your Dreams. Jewish Lights Publishing.

PSI Encyclopedia. https://psi-encyclopedia.spr.ac.uk /articles/dream-incubation.

The Real Samizdat. https://therealsamizdat.com /category/lailamchouch/.

Sacred-Texts.com. https://www.sacred-texts.com/egy /ema/ema09.htm.

3. dreams across cultures

Bahr, Donald. (1994). "Native American Dream Songs, Myth, Memory, and Improvisation." Journal de la Société des Americanistes, 73–93.

Boyer, Corinne. (2022). Dream Divination Plants. Three Hands Press.

Broad, William J. (2007). The Oracle: Ancient Delphi and the Science Behind Its Lost Secrets. Penguin.

Cacho, Valerie, & Green, Mindy. (2021). "Aromatherapy for Sleep." In Valerie Cacho & Esther Lum (Eds.), Integrative Sleep Medicine. Oxford University Press.

Campbell, Joseph. (2004). Pathways to Bliss: Mythology and Personal Transformation (Vol. 16). New World Library.

Campbell, Joseph. (2013). Goddesses: Mysteries of the Feminine Divine. Joseph Campbell Foundation.

Corbett, Lionel. (2002). The Religious Function of the Psyche. Routledge.

Daldianus, Artemidorus. (1990). The Interpretation of Dreams: Oneirocritica. (White, Robert John, Trans.) Original Books.

Doniger, Wendy (1999). "The Dreams and Dramas of a Jealous Hindu Queen." In Dream Cultures: Explorations in the Comparative History of Dreaming. Oxford University Press.

Duran, Eduardo, & Duran, Bonnie. (1995). Native American Postcolonial Psychology. Suny Press.

El-Kilany, Engy, & Elgammal, Islam. (2019). "Dream Incubation Tourism: The Resurrection of Ancient Egyptian Heritage of Sleep Temples." International Journal of Heritage and Museum Studies, 1(1).

Hammer, Jill. (2022). Undertorah: An Earth-Based Kabbalah of Dreams. Ayin Press.

Hillman, James, & Pierson, Fraser. (2010) Instructor's Manual for James Hillman on Archetypal Psychotherapy. Psychotherapy.net.

Hirst, Manton. (2005). "Dreams and Medicines: The Perspective of Xhosa Diviners and Novices in the Eastern Cape, South Africa." Indo-Pacific Journal of Phenomenology, 5(2), 1–22.

Ish-Shalom, Zvi. (2021). "Sleep, Death, and Rebirth." In Sleep, Death, and Rebirth. Academic Studies Press.

Kelsey, Morton T. (1978). Dreams: A Way to Listen to God. Paulist Press.

Kiefer, David. (2021). "Dietary and Herbal Supplements for Sleep." In Valerie Cacho & Esther Lum (Eds.), Integrative Sleep Medicine. Oxford University Press.

Moss, Robert. (2009). The Secret History of Dreaming. New World Library.

Norbu, Namkhai, & Katz, Michael. (1992). Dream Yoga and the Practice of Natural Light. Snow Lion Publications.

Ochs, Vanessa L., & Ochs, Elizabeth. (2003). The Jewish Dream Book: The Key to Opening the Inner Meaning of Your Dreams. Jewish Lights Publishing.

Shulman, David, & Stroumsa, Guy G. (1999). "Introduction." In D. Shulman & G. G. Stroumsa (Eds.), Dream Ccultures: Explorations in the Comparative History of Dreaming. Oxford University Press.

Sobiecki, Jean-Francois. (2008). "A review of plants used in divination in southern Africa and their psychoactive effects." Southern African Humanities, 20(2), 333–351.

Stevens, Anthony. (1997). Private Myths: Dreams and Dreaming. Harvard University Press.

Toro, Gianluca, & Thomas, Benjamin. (2007). Drugs of the Dreaming: Oneirogens: Salvia divinorum and Other Dream-Enhancing Plants. Simon and Schuster.

Vanderhooft, Eric. (2004). "Caduceus: The Staff of Asclepius or Hermes." The Pharos of Alpha Omega Alpha Honor Medical Society, 67(4), 22–26.

Van de Castle, Robert L. (1994). Our Dreaming Mind: A Sweeping Exploration of the Role that Dreams Have Played in Politics, Art, Religion, and Psychology, from Ancient Civilizations to the Present Day. Ballantine Books.

4. modern historical perspectives

Aizenstat, Stephen. https://dreamtending.com/dream-tending/.

Baraniuk, Chris. (2016) "The Enormous Power of the Unconscious Brain." BBC.com

Bettelheim, Bruno. (1983). Freud and Man's Soul: An Important Re-Interpretation of Freudian Theory. Vintage.

Brewster, Fanny. (2019). "Childhood Innocence: Racial Prejudice and the Shaping of Psychological Complexes." Psychological Perspectives, 62(2–3), 164–175.

Bury, Robert Gregg (Ed.). (1909). The Symposium of Plato. W. Heffer.

Frey-Rohn, Liliane. (1991). "How to Deal with Evil." In Zweig, Connie, & Abrams, Jeremiah. Meeting the Shadow: The Hidden Power of the Dark Side of Human Nature. Penguin.

Freud, Sigmund. (1965). The Interpretation of Dreams (J. Strachey, Trans.). Avon Books. (Original work published 1899.)

Hillman, James. (1975). Re-visioning Psychology. Harper & Row.

Jacobi, Jolande. (2013). Complex/Archetype/Symbol in the Psychology of CG Jung. Routledge.

Jung, Carl Gustav (1970). General Aspects of Dream Psychology. In The Collected Works of C. G. Jung: Vol. 8, The Structure & Dynamics of the Psyche. Princeton University Press.

Jung, Carl Gustav. (2014). Mysterium Coniunctionis: An Inquiry into the Separation and Synthesis of Psychic Opposites in Alchemy. Routledge. First published in 1963.

Jung, Carl Gustav. (1968). "The Concept of the Collective Unconscious" (R. F. C. Hull, Trans.). In H. Read et al. (Eds.), The Collected Works of C. G. Jung: Vol. 9, Part 1. Archetypes and the Collective Unconscious (2nd ed.). Princeton University Press. (Original work published 1936–1937.)

Reeves, Kenneth M. (2000). "Racism and Projection of the Shadow." Psychotherapy: Theory, Research, Practice, Training, 37(1).

Sharf, Richard S. (2015). Theories of Psychotherapy and Counseling: Concepts and Cases. Cengage Learning.

Stein, Murray. (1998). Jung's Map of the Soul: An "Introduction." Open Court Publishing.

von Franz, Marie-Louise (1980). Projection and Re-collection in Jungian Psychology: Reflections of the Soul. Open Court Publishing.

Whitmont, Edward C. (1991). "The Evolution of the Shadow." In Meeting the Shadow: The Hidden Power of the Dark Side of Human Nature. Jeremy P. Tarcher.

Woodman, Marion. (1993). "Conscious Femininity: Interviews with Marion Woodman" (Vol. 58). Studies in Jungian Psychology by Jungian Analysts.

Woodman, Marion, & Dickson, Elinor. (1996). Dancing in the Flames: The Dark Goddess in the Transformation of Consciousness. Shambhala Publications.

Zweig, Connie, & Abrams, Jeremiah. (1991). Meeting the Shadow: The Hidden Power of the Dark Side of Human Nature. Penguin.

5. the dreaming brain

Aspy, Denholm J. (2017). Studies for the Development of Effective Lucid Dream Induction Techniques (Doctoral dissertation).

Aspy, Denholm J., Delfabbro, Paul, Proeve, Michael, & Mohr, Philip. (2017). "Reality testing and the mnemonic induction of lucid dreams: Findings from the national Australian lucid dream induction study." Dreaming, 27(3), 206.

Becker, Udo. (Ed.). (2000). The Continuum Encyclopedia of Symbols. A&C Black.

Domhoff, G. William. (2003). The Scientific Study of Dreams: Neural Networks, Cognitive Development, and Content Analysis. American Psychological Association.

Jung, Carl Gustav, Adler, Gerhard, Fordham, Michael, & Read, Herbert. (2014). The Structure and Dynamics of the Psyche. Routledge.

Hobson, John Allan. (1988). The Dreaming Brain. Basic Books.

Hoel, Erik. (2021). "The Overfitted Brain: Dreams Evolved to Assist Generalization." Patterns, 2(5), 100244.

Naiman, Rubin. (2021). "Integrative Dream Medicine."
In Valerie Cacho & Esther Lum (Eds.), Integrative Sleep
Medicine. Oxford University Press.

Patel, Smita. (2021). "Sleep Hygiene." In Valerie Cacho
& Esther Lum (Eds.), Integrative Sleep Medicine. Oxford
University Press.

Solms, Mark. (2001). "The Interpretation of Dreams
and the Neurosciences." Psychoanalysis and History,
3(1), 79–91

Voss, Ursula, Holzmann, Romain, Hobson, John Allan,
Paulus, Walter, Koppehele-Gossel, Judith, Klimke,
Ansgar, and Nitsche, Michael A. (2014) "Induction of
self awareness in dreams through frontal low current
stimulation of gamma activity." Nature Neuroscience
17(6), 810–812.

Walker, Matthew. (2017). Why Your Brain Needs to Dream.
Greater Good Magazine.

6. working with your dreams

Andrews, Ted. (2010). Animal Speak: The Spiritual &
Magical Powers of Creatures Great and Small. Llewellyn
Worldwide.

Antoniou, Stavros A., Antoniou, George A., Learney,
Robert, Granderath, Frank A., & Antoniou,
Athanasios I. (2011). "The rod and the serpent: History's
ultimate healing symbol." World Journal of Surgery, 35(1),
217–221.

Barraniuk, Chris. (2016). The Enormous Power of the
Unconscious Brain. https://www.bbc.com/future/article
/20160315-the-enormous-power-of-the-unconscious
-brain.

Becker, Udo. (Ed.). (2000). The Continuum Encyclopedia of
Symbols. A&C Black.

Birnbaum, Lucia Chiavola. (1993). Black Madonnas:
Feminism, Religion, and Politics in Italy. Northeastern
University Press.

Blackie, Sharon. (2016). If Women Rose Rooted: A Life-
Changing Journey to Authenticity and Belonging. September
Publishing.

Bosnak, Robert. (1998). A Little Course in Dreams.
Shambhala.

Bosnak, Robert. (2007). Embodiment: Creative Imagination
in Medicine, Art and Travel. Routledge.

Brannen, Cyndi. (2019). Keeping Her Keys: An Introduction
to Hekate's Modern Witchcraft. John Hunt Publishing.

Brinton Perera, Sylvia. (1981). Descent to the Goddess: A
Way of Initiation for Women. Inner City.

Bulkeley, Kelly. (2016). Big Dreams: The Science of
Dreaming and the Origins of Religion. Oxford University
Press.

Campbell, Joseph. (2000). As cited in Grof, Stanislav,
Psychology of the Future: Lessons from Modern Consciousness
Research. State University of New York Press.

Camic, Paul. (1999). "Expanding treatment possibilities
for chronic pain through the expressive arts." In C.
Malchiodi (Ed.), Medical Art Therapy with Adults. Jessica
Kingsley.

Carus, Paul. (1900). Eros and Psyche: A Fairy-tale of Ancient
Greece. Open Court Publishing Company.

Castaneda, Carlos, & Moreno, Luis. (1993). The Art of
Dreaming. HarperCollins.

Chávez-Eakle, Rosa Aurora, Graff-Guerrero, Ariel,
García-Reyna, Juan-Carlos, Vaugier, Victor, & Cruz-
Fuentes, Carlos. (2007). "Cerebral blood flow associated
with creative performance: A comparative study."
Neuroimage, 38(3), 519–528.

Chilton, Gioia. (2013). "Art Therapy and Flow: A Review
of the Literature and Applications." Art Therapy, 30(2),
64–70.

Chodorow, Joan. (1997). "Introduction." In J. Chodorow
(Ed.), Jung on Active Imagination. Princeton University
Press.

Comas-Díaz, Lillian. (2003). The Black Madonna:
The Psychospiritual Feminism of Guadeloupe, Kali,
and Monserrat. In Louise B. Silverstein & Thelma J.
Goodrich (Eds.), Feminist Family Therapy: Empowerment
in Social Context. American Psychological Association.

Cseh, Genevieve M., Phillips, Louise H., & Pearson,
David G. (2015). "Flow, affect and visual creativity."
Cognition and Emotion, 29(2), 281–291.

Csikszentmihalyi, Mihaly. (1975). Beyond Boredom and
Anxiety: Experiencing Flow in Work and Play. Jossey-Bass.

Dalmiya, Vrinda. (2000). "Loving Paradoxes: A Feminist Reclamation of the Goddess Kali." *Hypatia*, 15(1), 125–150.

Dietrich, Arne. (2009). "The Transient Hypofrontality Theory and Its Implications for Emotion and Cognition." In Terry McMorris, Phillip D. Tomporowski, & Michel Audiffren (Eds.), *Exercise and Cognitive Function*. Wiley-Blackwell.

Dirkx, John M. (2000). *Transformative Learning and the Journey of Individuation* (ED448305). ERIC. https://files .eric.ed.gov/fulltext/ED448305.pdf.

Domash, Leanne. (2016). "Dreamwork and Transformation: Facilitating Therapeutic Change Using Embodied Imagination." *Contemporary Psychoanalysis*, 52(3), 410–433.

Edinger, Edward F., and Joan Dexter Blackmer. (1994) *Mystery of the Coniunctio: Alchemical*. Inner City Books.

Eller, Cynthia. (2000). "White Women and the Dark Mother." *Religion*, 30(4), 367–378.

Estés, Clarissa Pinkola. (1995). *Women Who Run with the Wolves: Myths and Stories of the Wild Woman Archetype*. Ballantine Books.

Firestone, Tirzah. (2022). *Wounds into Wisdom: Healing Intergenerational Jewish Trauma*. Monkfish Book Publishing.

Freeman, John. (1964). "Introduction." In C. G. Jung & M.-L. von Franz (Eds.), *Man and His Symbols*. Doubleday.

Gadon, Elinor W. (2002). "Probing the Mysteries of the Hirapur Yoginis." *Revision*, 25(1), 33–42.

Gillespie, Barry. (2014). Quoted in Kim Lim (Ed.), *1,001 Pearls of Spiritual Wisdom: Words to Enrich, Inspire, and Guide Your Life*. Skyhorse.

Gimbutas, Marija. (1981). "The 'Monstrous Venus' of Prehistory of Goddess Creatix." *Comparative Civilizations Review*, 7(7), 2.

Gray, Kurt, Anderson, Stephen, Chen, Eric Evan, Kelly, John Michael, Christian, Michael S., Patrick, John, Huang, Laura, Kenett Yoed N., & Lewis, Kevin. (2019). "'Forward flow': A New Measure to Quantify Free Thought and Predict Creativity." *American Psychologist*, 74(5), 539–554.

Grosch, William N., & Olsen, David C. (1994). *When Helping Starts to Hurt: A New Look at Burnout Among Psychotherapists*. W. W. Norton & Co.

Handy, Amy, & Strickland, Carol. (2001). *The Annotated Arch: A Crash Course in the History of Architecture* (Vol. 2). Andrews McMeel Publishing.

Harding, Esther. (2017). *Woman's Mysteries: Ancient & Modern*. Shambhala Publications.

Hartowicz, Sylvia Zofia. (2018). *Bringing Intergenerational Trauma and Resilience to Consciousness: The Journey of Healing and Transformation for the Wounded Healer Exploring Ancestral Legacy*. California Institute of Integral Studies.

Henderson, Joseph Lewis, and Maud Oakes. (1990). *The Wisdom of the Serpent: The Myths of Death, Rebirth, and Resurrection*. Vol. 648. Princeton University Press.

Hillman, James. (1977). "An Inquiry into Image." *Spring: An Annual of Archetypal Psychology and Jungian Thought*, 62–88. Spring Publications.

Hillman, James. (1975). *Re-visioning Psychology*. HarperCollins.

Hobson, John Allan. (1988). *The Dreaming Brain*. Basic Books.

Hopcke, H. Robert. (1999) *A Guided Tour of the Collected Works of C. G. Jung*. Shambhala Publications, Inc.

Horkey, Jess. (@bloodmilk). (2021). "Self-Portrait in the Labyrinth WIP." Instagram, September , 2021. https://www.instagram.com/p/CTX8HlCH9zO/?igshid =MDM4ZDc5MmU=.

Ish-Shalom, Zvi. (2017). *The Kedumah Experience: The Primordial Torah*. Albion-Andalus, Incorporated.

Johnson, Robert A. (1986). *Inner Work: Using Dreams and Active Imagination for Personal Growth*. HarperCollins.

Jung, Carl Gustav. (1971). *The Collected Works of C. G. Jung: Vol. 6. Psychological Types* (R. F. C. Hull, Trans.) (H. Read et al., Eds.). Princeton University Press. (Original work published 1921.)

Jung, Carl Gustav. (1966). *Collected Works of CG Jung, Volume 16: Practice of Psychotherapy*. Princeton University Press.

Jung, Carl Gustav. (1984). *Dream Analysis, Volume I: Seminars* (Vol. 1). Princeton University Press.

Jung, Carl Gustav. (1974). *Dreams* (R. F. C. Hull, Trans.). Princeton University Press.

Jung, Carl Gustav. (1997). *Jung on Active Imagination* (J. Chodorow, Ed.). Princeton University Press.

Jung, Carl Gustav, von Franz, Marie-Louise, Henderson, Joseph L., Jaffé, Aniela, & Jacobi, Jolande. (1964). *Man and His Symbols* (Vol. 5183). Dell.

Jung, Carl Gustav. (1963). *Memories, Dreams, Reflections* (Aniela Jaffé, Ed.) (Richard Winston & Clara Winston, Trans.). Pantheon Books. (Original work published 1961.)

Jung, Carl Gustav. (1969). "A Psychological Approach to the Dogma of the Trinity" (R. F. C. Hull, Trans.). In H. Read et al. (Eds.), *The Collected Works of C. G. Jung: Vol. 11. Psychology and Religion* (2nd ed.). Princeton University Press. (Original work published 1948.)

Jung, Carl Gustav. (1932). *Psychological Types*. Pantheon Books.

Jung, Carl Gustav. (2009). *The Red Book: Liber Novus* (Sonu Shamdasani, Ed. & Trans.; Mark Kyburz & John Peck, Trans.). W. W. Norton & Co.

Kalsched, Donald. (2014). *The Inner World of Trauma: Archetypal Defences of the Personal Spirit*. Routledge.

Kerényi, Karl. (1959). "Asklepios: Archetypal Image of the Physician's Existence." *Archetypal Images of Greek Religion*, 3.

Khodarahimi, Sidamak. (2010, September). "Snake Mother Imagery in Generalized Anxiety Disorder." In *International Forum of Psychoanalysis*, 19(3), 165–171.

Kotler, Steven. (2014). *The Rise of Superman: Decoding the Science of Ultimate Human Performance*. Houghton Mifflin Harcourt.

Kotler, Steven, & Wheal, Jamie. (2017). *Stealing Fire: How Silicon Valley, the Navy SEALs, and Maverick Scientists Are Revolutionizing the Way We Live and Work*. HarperCollins.

Kramer, Edith. (2001). "Sublimation and Art Therapy." In J. A. Rubin (Ed.), *Approaches to Art Therapy: Theory and Technique* (2nd ed.). Routledge.

Laios, K., Moschos, M. M., Koukaki, E., Vasilopoulos, E., Karamanou, M., Kontaxaki, M. I., & Androutsos, G. (2016). "Dreams in Ancient Greek Medicine." *Psychiatrikē Psychiatriki*, 27(3), 215–221.

Leeming, David Adams, Madden, Kathryn Wood, and Marlan, Stanton. (Eds.). (2014). *Encyclopedia of Psychology and Religion*. Springer.

Lusebrink, Vija B. (2004). "Art Therapy and the Brain: An Attempt to Understand the Underlying Processes of Art Expression in Therapy." *Art Therapy*, 21(3), 125–135.

Mahantesh, Vijay Gurumurthy. (2018). *Kali, Shiva, and Psychotherapy: A Hermeneutic Literature Review*. (Doctoral dissertation, Auckland University of Technology.)

Malchiodi, Cathy A. (2011a). "Art Therapy and the Brain." In Cathy A. Malchiodi (Ed.), *Handbook of Art Therapy*. Guilford Press.

Malchiodi, Cathy A. (2011b). "Art Therapy in Practice: Ethics, Evidence and Cultural Sensitivity." In Cathy A. Malchiodi (Ed.), *Handbook of Art Therapy*. Guilford Press.

Malchiodi, Cathy A. (2011c). "Art Therapy: Materials, Media and Methods." In C. A. Malchiodi (Ed.), *Handbook of Art Therapy*. Guilford Press.

McNiff, Shaun. (1992). *Art as Medicine: Creating a Therapy of the Imagination*. Shambhala Publications.

Meier, Carl Alfred. (2009). *Healing Dream and Ritual: Ancient Incubation and Modern Psychotherapy*. Daimon.

Mellick, Jill. (2001). *The Art of Dreaming: Tools for Creative Dream Work*. Conari Press.

Meyer, Kenneth. (2016). "Gestalt Dreamwork." In J. E. Lewis & S. Krippner (Eds.), *Working with Dreams and PTSD Nightmares: 14 Approaches for Psychotherapists and Counselors*. ABC-CLIO.

Mezzatesta, Heidi. (2021). *What the Witch Knows: A Hermeneutic Depth Psychological Examination of the Salem Trials*. (Dissertation, Pacifica Graduate Institute.)

McCurdy, Jole. (1991). "The Structural and Archetypal Analysis of Fairy Tales." *Psyche's Stories: Modern Jungian Interpretations of Fairy Tales*. Nicolas-Hays, Inc.

McLean, Adam. (1989). *The Triple Goddess: An Exploration of the Archetypal Feminine* (Vol. 1). Red Wheel/Weiser.

Montijo, Mark. (2020) *Lecture on Archetypes as We Age*. Pacifica Graduate Institute.

Moon, Bruce L. (2007). The Role of Metaphor in Art Therapy: Theory, Method, and Experience. Charles C. Thomas Publisher.

Moss, Robert. (2009). The Secret History of Dreaming. New World Library.

Moss, Robert. (2010). Conscious Dreaming: A Spiritual Path for Everyday Life. Harmony.

Neumann, Erich. (1991). The Great Mother: An Analysis of the Archetype (R. Manheim, Trans.). Princeton University Press. (Original work published 1955.)

Online Etymology Dictionary. https://www.etymonline.com.

Pagel, James F., & Kwiatkowski, Carol F. (2003). "Creativity and dreaming: Correlation of reported dream incorporation into waking behavior with level and type of creative interest." Creativity Research Journal, 15(2–3), 199–205.

Papadopoulos, Renos K. (Ed.). (2006). The Handbook of Jungian Psychology: Theory, Practice and Applications. Psychology Press.

Perera, Sylvia Brinton. (1981). Descent to the Goddess: A Way of Initiation for Women. Inner City.

Plotkin, Bill. (2010). Soulcraft: Crossing into the Mysteries of Nature and Psyche. New World Library.

Reynolds, Frances, & Prior, Sarah. (2006). "Creative Adventures and Flow in Art-Making: A Qualitative Study of Women Living with Cancer." British Journal of Occupational Therapy, 69(6), 255–26.

Ronnberg, Anni, & Martin, Kathleen. (Eds.). (2010). The Book of Symbols. Taschen.

Russack, Neil W. (1984). "Amplification: The Spiral." Journal of Analytical Psychology, 29(2), 125–134.

Schaverien, Joy. (2005). "Art, dreams and active imagination: A post-Jungian approach to transference and the image." Journal of Analytical Psychology, 50(2), 127–153.

Sells, Benjamin. (Ed.). (2000). Working with Images: The Theoretical Base of Archetypal Psychology. Spring Publications.

Sharf, Richard S. (2015). Theories of Psychotherapy and Counseling: Concepts and Cases. Cengage Learning.

Sharp, Jonathan. (2010). Divining Your Dreams: How the Ancient, Mystical Tradition of the Kabbalah Can Help You Interpret 1,000 Dream Images. Simon and Schuster.

Shulman, David, & Stroumsa, Guy G. (1999). "Introduction." In D. Shulman & G. G. Stroumsa (Eds.), Dream Cultures: Explorations in the Comparative History of Dreaming. Oxford University Press.

Sollée, Kristen J. (2017). Witches, Sluts, Feminists: Conjuring the Sex Positive. Three L Media/Stonebridge Press.

Stein, Murray. (2006). "Individuation." In R. K. Papadopoulos (Ed.), The Handbook of Jungian Psychology: Theory, Practice and Applications. Routledge.

Stein, Murray. (1998). Jung's Map of the Soul: An "Introduction." Open Court Publishing.

Stein, Murray. (1998). Transformation: Emergence of the Self (No. 7). Texas A&M University Press.

Steiner, Rudolf. (1994). How to Know Higher Worlds: A Modern Path of Initiation. SteinerBooks.

Stevens, Anthony. (1997). Private Myths: Dreams and Dreaming. Harvard University Press.

Stevenson, Angus. (Ed.). (2010). Oxford Dictionary of English. Oxford University Press, USA.

Swan-Foster, Nora. (2018). Jungian Art Therapy: Images, Dreams, and Analytical Psychology. Routledge.

Thomas, R. Elizabeth, & Rappaport, Julian. (1996). "Art as Community Narrative: A Resource for Social Change." In M. B. Lykes, A. Banuazizi, M. Morris, & R. Liem (Eds.), Myths About the Powerless: Contesting Social Inequalities. Temple University Press.

Tsoucalas, Gregory, & Androutsos, George. (2019). "Asclepius and the Snake as Toxicological Symbols in Ancient Greece and Rome." In Toxicology in Antiquity. Academic Press.

Ulanov, Ann Barry. (1987). The Witch and the Clown: Two Archetypes of Human Sexuality. Chiron Publications.

Van de Castle, Robert L. (1994). Our Dreaming Mind: A Sweeping Exploration of the Role that Dreams Have Played in Politics, Art, Religion, and Psychology, from Ancient Civilizations to the Present Day. Ballantine Books.

Vanderhooft, Eric. (2004). "Caduceus: The Staff of Asclepius or Hermes." The Pharos of Alpha Omega Alpha Honor Medical Society, 67(4), 22–26.

Vass, Marc, Carroll, John M., & Shaffer, Clifford A. (2002). "Supporting Creativity in Problem Solving Environments." In Proceedings of the 4th Conference on Creativity & Cognition.

von Franz, Marie-Louise. (1994). Archetypal Dimensions of the Psyche. Shambhala Publications.

von Franz, Marie-Louise. (2012). "Dream of a Ten-Year-Old Girl of a Snake with Eyes Sparkling Like Diamonds." In Carl Gustav Jung, Children's Dreams: Notes from the Seminar Given in 1936–1940. Princeton University Press.

von Franz, Marie-Louise. (1996). The Interpretation of Fairy Tales. Shambhala Publications.

Wallas, Graham. (1926). The Art of Thought. Harcourt-Brace.

Whitmont, Edward C., & Perera, Sylvia Briton. (2013). Dreams, A Portal to the Source. Routledge.

Woodman, Marion, & Dickson, Elinor. (1996). Dancing in the Flames: The Dark Goddess in the Transformation of Consciousness. Shambhala Publications.

Young, Serinity. (2018). Women Who Fly: Goddesses, Witches, Mystics, and Other Airborne Females. Oxford University Press.

7. types of dreams

Aspy, Denholm J., Delfabbro, Paul, Proeve, Michael, & Mohr, Philip. (2017). "Reality testing and the mnemonic induction of lucid dreams: Findings from the national Australian lucid dream induction study." Dreaming, 27(3), 206.

Aspy, Denholm J. (2020). "Findings from the International Lucid Dream Induction Study." Frontiers in Psychology, 1746.

Castaneda, Carlos, & Moreno, Luis. (1993). The Art of Dreaming. HarperCollins.

Das, Lama Surya. (2000). Tibetan Dream Yoga: A Complete System for Becoming Conscious in Your Dreams. Sounds True.

Ellis, Leslie. (2019). A Clinician's Guide to Dream Therapy: Implementing Simple and Effective Dreamwork. Routledge.

Erlacher, Daniel, Stumbrys, Tadas, & Schredl, Michael. (2012). "Frequency of lucid dreams and lucid dream practice in German athletes." Imagination, Cognition and Personality, 31(3), 237–246.

Freud, Sigmund, & Strachey, James Ed. (1964). The Standard Edition of the Complete Psychological Works of Sigmund Freud. The Hogarth Press.

Holecek, Andrew. (2016). Dream Yoga: Illuminating Your Life Through Lucid Dreaming and the Tibetan Yogas of Sleep. Sounds True.

Jung, Carl Gustav. (1976). "Symbols and the Interpretation of Dreams." In H. Read et al. (Eds.), The Collected Works of C. G. Jung: Vol. 18. The Symbolic Life. Princeton University Press. (Original work published 1964.)

LaBerge, Stephen. (2003). "Lucid Dreaming and the Yoga of the Dream State: A Psychophysiological Perspective." Buddhism and Science: Breaking New Ground. Columbia University Press.

Moss, Robert. (2009). The Secret History of Dreaming. New World Library.

Moss, Robert. (2010). Conscious Dreaming: A Spiritual Path for Everyday Life. Harmony.

Naiman, Rubin. (2021). "Integrative Dream Medicine." In Valerie Cacho & Esther Lum (Eds.), Integrative Sleep Medicine. Oxford University Press.

Nielsen, Tore. (1988). "Ancient methods of dream incubation: Bodily methods of inducing spiritual presence." Bulletin of the Montreal Center for the Study of Dreams, 3(3–4), 6–10.

Norbu, Namkhai, & Katz, Michael. (1992). Dream Yoga and the Practice of Natural Light. Snow Lion Publications.

Rosenbusch, Kaylee Michael Ann. (2016). Lucid Dreaming: Exploring the Effects of Lucidity within Dreams on Emotion Regulation, Positive Emotions, Interoceptive Awareness, and Mindfulness. Arizona State University.

Schmitt, Jean Claude. (1999). "The Liminality and Centrality of Dreams in the Medieval West." Dream Cultures: Explorations in the Comparative History of Dreaming, 274. Oxford University Press.

von Nettesheim, Heinrich Cornelius Agrippa. (1993) Three Books of Occult Philosophy. Llewellyn Worldwide. (Originally published in 1651.)

Wallace, B. Alan, & Hodel, Brian. (2012). Dreaming Yourself Awake: Lucid Dreaming and Tibetan Dream Yoga for Insight and Transformation. Shambhala Publications.

Wangyal, Tenzin. (1998). The Tibetan Yogas of Dream and Sleep. Shambhala Publications.

8. nightmares

Allione, Tsultrim. (2008). Feeding Your Demons: Ancient Wisdom for Resolving Inner Conflict. Little, Brown Spark.

Aspy, Denholm J. (2017). Studies for the Development of Effective Lucid Dream Induction Techniques (Doctoral dissertation).

Aspy, Denholm J., Delfabbro, Paul, Proeve, Michael, & Mohr, Philip. (2017). "Reality testing and the mnemonic induction of lucid dreams: Findings from the national Australian lucid dream induction study." Dreaming, 27(3), 206.

Campbell, Joseph. (2008). The Hero with a Thousand Faces (Vol. 17). New World Library.

Coppola, Francis Ford, Oldman, Gary, Ryder, Winona, Hopkins, Anthony, & Hart, James V. (1992). Bram Stoker's Dracula. Sony Pictures Home Entertainment.

Hartmann, Ernest. (1989). "Boundaries of dreams, boundaries of dreamers: Thin and thick boundaries as a new personality measure." Psychiatric Journal of the University of Ottawa, 14(4), 557–560.

Hollis, James. (2008). Why Good People Do Bad Things: Understanding Our Darker Selves. Penguin.

Hurd, Ryan. (2010). Sleep Paralysis: A Guide to Hypnagogic Visions & Visitors of the Night. Hyena Press.

Johnson, Robert A. (1993). Owning Your Own Shadow: Understanding the Dark Side of the Psyche. Harper Collins.

Jung, Carl Gustav. (1968). "The Concept of the Collective Unconscious" (R. F. C. Hull, Trans.). In H. Read et al. (Eds.), The Collected Works of C. G. Jung: Vol. 9, Part 1. Archetypes and the Collective Unconscious (2nd ed.). Princeton University Press. (Original work published 1936–1937.)

Kunzendorf, Robert G., Hartmann, Ernest, Cohen, Rachel, & Cutler, Jennifer. (1997). "Bizarreness of the dreams and daydreams reported by individuals with thin and thick boundaries." Dreaming, 7(4), 265.

Leschziner, Guy. (2019). The Nocturnal Brain: Tales of Nightmares and Neuroscience. Simon and Schuster.

Michaels, Stase. (2018). Nightmares: The Dark Side of Dreams and Dreaming. Sterling Publishing Co.

Patel, Smita. (2021). "Sleep Hygiene." In Valerie Cacho & Esther Lum (Eds.), Integrative Sleep Medicine. Oxford University Press.

Rees, Oreet, & Whitney, Leanne. (2020). "The Sleep Paralysis Nightmare, Wrathful Deities, and the Archetypes of the Collective Unconscious." Psychological Perspectives, 63(1), 23–39.

Reeves, Kenneth M. (2000). "Racism and projection of the shadow." Psychotherapy: Theory, Research, Practice, Training, 37(1), 80.

Thalbourne, Michael A., & Maltby, John. (2008). "Transliminality, thin boundaries, unusual experiences, and temporal lobe lability." Personality and Individual Differences, 44(7), 1617–1623.

conclusion

Becker, Udo. (Ed.). (2000). The Continuum Encyclopedia of Symbols. A&C Black.

Grey, Peter. (2013). Apocalyptic Witchcraft. Scarlet Imprint.

ACKNOWLEDGMENTS

First and foremost, I would like to acknowledge my loving parents, Rick and Cindy, whose ability to alchemize conscious experience, do deep inner work, and show up as the most compassionate and wonderful people walking this green earth is my greatest blessing. Thank you for recording my dreams at one year of age and never ceasing to support my magic, growth, and twisting life's path. To my beloved partner, there is no way this book would have emerged from my psyche without your undying care and support; I cherish you beyond death. Thank you for your brilliance, for never doubting me, and for being by my side always, in all ways. Thank you to my dear sister, for your existence is a constant inspiration to my highest expression. Thank you to all my therapists, Jungian analysts, teachers, and mentors for your wisdom, guidance, and profound jewels of insight; I dearly treasure each of you. Thank you to my amazing Ritualcravt family, for believing in me since the beginning and supporting my work across dimensions; I love you all to the moon.

Thank you to my phenomenal literary agent, Adriana Stimola, for your tireless enthusiasm, fervor, and confidence from this project's inception and throughout its birth process. Thank you to my marvelous editor Kate Zimmermann, for discovering my writing and pulling this book out of the recesses of my soul, for reading and rereading my flowery language, and for working with me to truly make my dreams come true. I want to express my deepest gratitude to all of the previously mentioned and credited art therapists, depth psychologists, Jungian analysts, artists, dreamers, and true visionaries, as well as thank all of the witches, queers, writers, occultists, thinkers, movers, and shakers; this world needs you. I extend my greatest appreciation, reverence, and awe to all the wild women who refuse to be silenced and to my matrilineal line of witchy individuals who have worked timelessly to carve the way for powerful unconscious and feminine wisdom. And lastly, but most notably, to my ancestors, for without you I would not exist; I cherish and honor you through my life and my work.

ABOUT THE AUTHOR

Naomi Sangreal is an avid dreamer, artist, Jewish witch, and magical psycho-therapist. She holds an MA in Counseling and Depth Psychology from Pacifica Graduate Institute, and a BA in Transpersonal Psychology and Art Therapy from Naropa University. Since 2017, Sangreal has been a resident consulting intuitive and dream specialist teaching at Ritualcravt, Denver's premier witchcraft shop, where she's offered a variety of courses on dreams, nightmares, and shadow work. Sangreal was born and raised in Southeast Portland, Oregon, and grew up somewhere in the crossfire of Kabbalistic mysticism, former Deadheads, radical feminists, and the West Coast punk scene, and her work as a therapist and an artist draws on, and extends beyond, her roots. Sangreal is both formally trained as an oil painter and an autodidact; she spent some time at the Pacific Northwest College of Art, but even more in the Victorian attics and concrete basements she's called her studios. Sangreal's passion for art is only matched by her fascina-tion with magic and the human mind. With one foot in each world, she brings together the healing power of psychology and the transformative wisdom of spirit to artfully guide her clients through life's challenges.